Make the money and run

The **YES** Series

Make the money and run

18 Businesses to Make You Rich

Siriol Jameson
Dash-Hill, LLC, Las Vegas, Nevada

Make the money and run: 18 Business to Make You Rich

Published by:
 Dash-Hill, LLC
 Las Vegas, NV
 www.dashhillpress.com

All rights reserved under International and Pan-American Copyright Conventions. No part of this book may be reproduced or transmitted in whole or in part in any form or by any means, electronic or mechanical, including photocopying, recording or by an information and retrieval system without explicit written permission of the publisher. Translation of any part of this work beyond that permitted by the Copyright Law without explicit written permission of the publisher is unlawful.

Copyright © 2001
First Printing 2001
Printed in the United States of America

To order:
Please order additional copies of this book at your favorite bookstore or call toll free: 1 (800) 247-6553

Publisher's Cataloging-in-Publication
(Provided by Quality Books, Inc.)

Jameson, Siriol.
    Make the money and run : 18 businesses to make you rich / Siriol Jameson. -- 1st ed.
      p. cm. -- (The YES series)
      Includes bibliographical references and index.
      LCCN: 00-090387
      ISBN: 0-9679432-1-3

    1. New business enterprises. 2. Success in business.
3. Small business. I. Title.

HD62.5.J36 2001   658.1'1
                        QBI01-200131

***Dedicated to William and Julia Sharp,
Benedict F. Manovill
and to my readers***

Current titles from The YES Series:

Make the money and run: 18 Businesses to Make You Rich

Forthcoming titles from The YES Series:

Easy Money: How to Get Rich in the Home Security Business

How the Gladiators Got Thin: Amazing Secrets of Losing Weight

Notice

This publication is intended to provide accurate and authoritative information in regard to the subject matter covered. It is distributed with the understanding that the publisher and the author, or their assignees or licensees, are not engaged in rendering legal or other professional services or advice. If legal or other expert assistance is required, the services of a competent professional should be sought.

The publisher and author, or their assignees or licensees, cannot guarantee specific results in connection with this guide as individual situations differ. Use this guide for general information only. Do not rely on it for a specific case.

This publication is intended to inform and entertain. The publisher and author, or their assignees or licensees, disclaim any personal loss or liability caused in connection with the use of information provided in this publication. Nor shall they be held liable for any commercial damage, including but not limited to special, incidental, consequential or other damages of any kind.

The publisher and author, and their assignees or licensees, assume no responsibility for the reliability of sources mentioned in this book. Mistakes do occur and there may be some in the book's information. The information is current up to the book's printing date. Nor do they make any representations or warranties as to the completeness or accuracy of the information. They disclaim any implied warranties or merchantability or fitness for a particular purpose. Any advice, opinions or claims implied or expressed in this publication do not constitute a guarantee. Brand names, proper names and descriptions are used for illustrative purposes only.

Contents

Preface – Look Who Made It ix

Part I: How to Be Your Own Boss 1

Introduction - You've Got What It Takes 3
The A-B-C's of Starting Your Business 7
7 Keys to Success 19

Part II: Which Business? 25

1. Your Man in Rio 27
2. Gift Albums 37
3. Lighting Specialist 45
4. Import - Export 53
5. Newsletter 63
6. Mail Order 71
7. Dating Service 79
8. Pet Boarding 87
9. Homemade Booklets 95
10. Wellness Specialist 103
11. Private Detective 113
12. Place a Chef 121

13. Diaries 129
14. Trade Shows 137
15. Regulations Specialist 145
16. Nonprofit 153
17. Information Broker 161
18. Executive Coach 167

Part III: Succeeding in Business 175

Marketing is Magic 177
Secrets of Doubling ... or Tripling Your Profits ... 191
A Parting Thought 199

Appendix 201

Business Launching Checklist 203
Publications 205
Resources 211
Government Help 215
Government Publications 219

Glossary 221

Bibliography 239

Index 241

PREFACE – LOOK WHO MADE IT

I have a message for you from a soldier.

His name is Will. Like most of us, Will has seen more bad times than good. He came back from a mission with ruined eyes. The doctors did what they could. Soon, though, they removed one of Will's eyes. After that, the other eye went blind.

He didn't want to live on disability so he searched for a job. He had an MBA. But it turned out that no company wanted a blind man. Still, there was no question in his mind that he would make it on his own.

So he decided to go into business for himself.

He used his small savings to live on while he searched for opportunities. He saw some of his blind friends go into business. A few were soldiers like he was. One ran a self service laundry. Another sold big appliances.

Will did succeed. And, he wants to give you this message:

"I made it without eyes. If you can see, you're already way ahead of the game."

PART I

How to Be Your Own Boss

Handwritten notes at top:
LOCATION — 300 ~~~~ ~~~
S-Corporations ———— , Name
Incorporate in:
address: Home, (as long as possible) — then: tiny office.
Hire person to answer tel:
— state

Introduction – You've Got What It Takes

You are an opportunity bringer. *(Really?)*

By following the steps in this guide and starting your own business, you could bring opportunities to everyone. You could earn enough money to open up a new world for you and your family. Your product might enrich the lives of your customers. And you may be in a position to offer people jobs.

(Really? ?) You have everything it takes to go into business now. Everything you have ever done in life has prepared you for this moment. Your successes have built up your confidence. Your hardships have toughened you. *you sure?*

The businesses in this guide are real. Any one of them could make you a great deal of money. I have been connected with a number of them and I have interviewed people who were successful in them.

Plus that, these businesses are fun to operate. Think of yourself dining on the Orient Express after having completed a business deal in Paris. If this idea appeals to you, read the chapters, "Your Man in Rio,"

4   Make the Money and Run

"Import-Export" or "Mail Order."
If investigations are more your style, perhaps the chapter on "Private Detective" would interest you. Investigating information is the lifeblood of the work of the information broker and that is described in its own chapter.

Some of the businesses are unusual. In fact, so unusual that you may not of heard of them. And yet, these unheard-of businesses can make you richer than you might have dreamed.

Read about some of these unheard-of businesses in the chapters: "Gift Albums" and "Diaries." They are very real. There are people who are making a fortune in them. When you read about them you will realize how easy it would be for you to make huge profits, too.

In addition to the 18 powerful businesses, examine the 57 related businesses. These are just as high-profit. They include: "Food delivery from area restaurants," "Personal chef," "Mail order catalogues," "Export management" and "International trade consultant." Keep in mind that old *80-20 rule*, though. It says that 20 percent of your customers will bring in 80 percent of the money. Always keep on the side of that 20 percent. If you find that 20 percent in a related business, put all your effort into it.

Once your main business takes off and you are making a lot of money, why not open another one. A man across the street from me just bought a copy shop. By training, he's an optician so he also sells eyeglasses in the same shop. His main business remains the copy shop because that is where the big money is.

A person I found out about in San Diego started out selling baby carriages. But he branched out into food shops, pet supplies and American craft figures. I don't know if he is using the *80-20 rule* or not, but I know he's having fun.

What a time to be alive!

Opportunities are circling us like stars. It's up to us to each out and grasp them.

How do you know which opportunity to grasp?

Go into something you like doing. If you like animals, open a pet boarding or pet sitting service. If travel attracts you, try import-export. To get some ideas, visit trade shows and look at all the products you think you could sell. Go into mail order. Why not start a catalogue? Catalogue sales are booming. Sell online. And, sell to the government.

While searching for a product or service, look for something that is a repeat seller. Cookbooks, horoscopes, software, puzzles, games, kitchen utensils and greeting cards sell and sell again to the same customers.

Another good strategy is to sell a product that ties in with another product. For instance, your good customer will be glad to buy your new cutting board. It will go with the salad bowl you already sold him.

Collectibles are selling like hotcakes. Choose one or two items and concentrate on them. To see what is popular, check ads in the magazines at the check-out counter of your supermarket and in the magazine section of the Sunday paper. There is no need to go it alone, either. Join a trade association, the Chamber of Commerce or a merchants' association. Even the federal government will help. They have experts who

6 Make the Money and Run

will sit down with you and advise you about what to do. It is all free of charge.

If you are near a university, go to the School of Business Administration and ask for assistance from graduate students. They are called "interns." You pay them nothing. They get credit from the school for work experience. Thus, you get top-notch help free.

Look through the businesses in this guide. Find three or four that sound interesting. Go through the list of resources at the end of each chapter and call or write the contacts you find there.

Now is the time to use my success formula. Write down your answers to the following questions:

What is my product?
Who are my buyers?
Who is going to help me sell my product?

You have just written your easy business plan. This formula is simple and powerful. It will help guide you to the right business. And once you are in business, keep the formula handy. It will keep you on the right track.

And now, let's get started. Keep this guide by your side. Follow it step by step.

When you have doubts and don't think you can make it, think of Will's message from the Preface of this guide:

"If you can see, you're already way ahead of the game!"

The A-B-C's of Starting Your Business

Setting up business is simple. People think it's hard because of all the misleading information about how to do it. Here's a look at how easy it really is.

First, decide which business structure you want.

BUSINESS STRUCTURE [LLC]

You can organize your business in five ways: a sole proprietorship, a general partnership, a C corporation, an S corporation or a limited liability company.

SOLE PROPRIETORSHIP

This is the simplest business structure. There are only two steps to set it up. They are:
- Check with the county clerk to see if you need a license in your area.

- File a fictitious name, or *DBA*, with the county clerk.

DBA stands for "doing business as." This records the name of the business and who owns it. You are given a DBA certificate.

The sole proprietorship costs little to set up. You are taxed only once and that is on your personal income tax. The big drawbacks are that you can be sued for anything your company does. And you're responsible for its debts.

GENERAL PARTNERSHIP

If you go into business with others, you might choose a general partnership. It's risky though. Each person is liable for the actions of all the others—and their debts.

The partnership's great advantage, though, is that income is passed through directly to the partners. That way, it is taxed at their individual level. The partnership itself pays no tax.

Neither the partnership nor the sole proprietorship enjoy the exciting fringe benefits that the next three business structures have.

C CORPORATION

A regular corporation is called a C corporation. It's a separate entity much like another person. It is liable for its own actions and debts. You, as the owner, are legally an employee of the corporation. You are protected from the debts of your business.

The benefits of a corporation are extraordinary.

For instance, you can buy equipment and lease it to your corporation. The money the corporation pays you is written off as a rental expense. Then you depreciate the equipment on your personal tax return. Also, there are medical and retirement benefits. And bonuses and free travel.

Which business structure is the best? That depends on you but I recommend the next two. The S corporation and the limited liability company, or LLC.

S Corporation

The S corporation is ideal. You're in business for yourself. You have all the benefits of the biggest corporations in the world, yet you don't have to pay a corporate tax. Instead, profits and losses are passed to you personally. This advantage is not given to the big corporations.

The earnings of S corporations are taxed only once. C corporations' earnings are taxed two times— once as corporate income and again as dividend income.

Think of the powerful fringe benefits a big corporation gives you. The S corporation gives the same benefits. It will pay medical insurance. You can put away large amounts of money for retirement. You are not liable for the corporation's acts. There are many tax breaks. Plus, it's easier for an S or a C corporation to borrow money than it is for a sole proprietorship or a partnership.

LIMITED LIABILITY COMPANY

The limited liability company, or LLC, is wildly popular. And it is simple. It lets you keep more money and shields you from lawsuits just like a corporation.

The LLC pays no federal income tax. It acts like a partnership or an S corporation. Income is passed through directly to you and you include it on your personal income tax return.

Generally, the LLC is used in place of a partnership. That is, it is set up with two persons, or members, as they are called in an LLC. But many states allow one person, or a sole proprietor, to set up a sole-member LLC.

Check the rules in your state for LLCs. On the whole, an LLC offers all the advantages of corporations and partnerships.

HOW TO SET UP YOUR BUSINESS

You can set up a sole proprietorship on your own. It costs very little. Contact the county clerk.

Have a lawyer set up your partnership or LLC.

A C corporation or an S corporation can be set up cheaply by going through an incorporation service. The service does all the work.

Incorporate your business in Nevada. There are no state taxes and the privacy laws are excellent. Wyoming is also good.

NAMING YOUR BUSINESS

Give a lot of thought to this. You'll use the name of your company a hundred times a day. Say it out loud. How does it sound? Is it easy to remember? Does it sound like a big company?

Your business name will be on your business bank account... on the radio... in the paper... on a bus bench.

I took a lot of time to find a name for my business. Finally, I chose "Dash," my dog's name. And "Hill" is short for "Whittington Hill, a place that still has a pharmacy with a soda fountain and big, old houses shaded by oak trees.

Choose a place name or pet name like I did, or use a name that projects an image of what you do or sell, such as "Thirsty Mops" or "Strong Arm Vaults."

Many people use their own name for their business. Don't make this mistake. Legally, you cannot protect your own name. Someone else may have your name and compete with you. Also, if the business fails or is sued, your name loses value. Plus, it makes it sound like a small business.

Just as with your own name, you cannot protect a *descriptive* name. A descriptive name is something like "lite" or "digital."

When choosing a name, think of your future customers. Are they old, young, rich, adventurous? What name would attract them?

Try to avoid names that sound or look like famous brands or companies. It is an invitation to a lawsuit.

One person I know considers *eight* his lucky number. He picks names with eight letters. He counts the name alone—such as "Pickwick"—but not the word after it, such as "Publishers," or "Inc."

Some people use a name beginning with "A," so they will be at the beginning of a directory. Notice how many businesses have names beginning with "A-AA," or "A-1" so they will be first on any list.

Once you have chosen the name, do a name search. If the name has not been taken, file an application for it. You do not need a lawyer.

YOUR BUSINESS ADDRESS

Your address, like your name, is supremely important. A local address inspires trust. Use a street address rather than a post office box address.

It's not necessary to use your home address. In fact, it's better not to unless you have a place to receive customers.

A good choice is a private mailbox service. Use their street address. Place the box number at the end of the street address. Let's say the box number happens to be 112. Show it in your address as: No. 112.

If you do expect to receive customers, a good location is vital. Choose an area where your competition is. Customers also want parking.

Some businesses require an upscale location. An example is a dating service. Location is more important than size. Customers will happily squeeze into a tiny shop.

RESALE NUMBER

The state issues this number. With it, you pay no sales tax for products you intend to resell. You also pay no tax on raw materials you use to make a product for sale. *How about added value?*

AN OFFICE

I'm often asked if it's important to rent an office. My answer is: "No."

This reminds me of an office designer in California who inherited $90,000. She rented a large storefront on the main shopping street. It had nine or ten model offices inside. Customers were supposed to walk through and choose an office for her to set up for them.

Months went by. She had a lot of walk-throughs but no clients. Soon the money was gone and she was forced to take out a loan. In the end, she went out of business. And she still had two years left on the lease.

Many business owners make the same mistake she did. Try not to pay rent unless you absolutely have to. Set up in the garage. That way you really are away at work when friends drop in. Rent a workroom at a monastery or in a college library. Or use a spare bedroom at home.

INSURANCE

Before doing any business at all—buy insurance. You'll need it against liability, theft, disability and fire. It's a big up-front cost but worth every penny.

Businesses are sued without merit every day. A frivolous suit can put you out of business—or worse. It's too late to buy insurance after you are sued.

Many people put off buying business insurance. They think their homeowner's policy is enough. It isn't. Most homeowner's policies don't cover you if, for example, a deliveryman falls carrying supplies for you into the garage. Riders on a homeowner's policy aren't enough.

Some states offer a mini-business owner's package policy. Some are good deals but often require you to buy homeowners' and auto policies from them as well.

Check out independent agents who specialize in small businesses. They can usually get the best rates available. The good thing is they work for you—not the insurance company.

Start out by contacting your trade association and suppliers. Both may offer package policies. Usually, the policy they offer is less expensive and it offers exactly the right coverage for your business.

Shop around before you make your decision. Rates vary on everything except workers compensation. Ask business owners in your area which insurance company they deal with. Find out if they are satisfied. Also, check the Internet for insurers.

LAWYER

Take time to choose a lawyer. Ask other tradespeople for referrals. Ask your trade association, suppliers and accountant.

Go to the library and look up lawyers specializing in small business. You can find them in *Martindale-Hubbell Law Directory*. Interview five or six lawyers. Ask for a free initial consultation.

You want a lawyer you can get along with. You should also be able to reach him or her when you need to. He or she must be dependable. You do not want to be abandoned in a crisis.

Once you've narrowed the list down to two or three, check them out. Call your state's Bar Association, the Office of the Attorney General, the Better Business Bureau and the Chamber of Commerce.

ACCOUNTANT

You probably won't need a CPA right away. Accountants do a good job for less money. They not only keep your books, they save you money. They help you take advantage of little-known tax deductions. They avoid sending up red flags that attract an audit. And, they send in quarterly taxes on time.

A beginning accountant charges so little it simply isn't worth doing the work yourself. *They probably make more mistakes, too!*

SUPPLIER

Be a partner to your suppliers. When you find good ones, stay with them. Don't jump around.

There are three types:

Manufacturers. They make the product. You have to buy a lot of units to get a low price.

Importers. They also deal in large orders.

Distributors. They're the best for beginners. Most have a low or no minimum purchase and prices are low.

Work out a *lead time*. This is the time it takes for you to get supplies. It could be a day or a month. If the lead time is long, build up an inventory for three months.

Bargain when buying supplies. Never accept a price quote. Don't pay sales tax if you have a tax exemption certificate. Remember to ask your supplier about returns.

The supplier may request immediate payment for the first few orders. After that, ask for a line of credit. Request a discount if you pay within ten days. Pay suppliers promptly and use them as a reference to get a line of credit with others.

As a precaution, always have a back-up supplier who can fill your order in case your primary supplier cannot deliver.

Ask suppliers for easy payment terms, customer leads, video sales materials and express service. They may also be able to get you vehicles, tools and office supplies at big discounts.

Your suppliers want you to succeed.

LETTERHEAD

Be conservative. Hire a professional to design your letterhead. Use black or blue ink.

If you belong to a trade association, the Better Business Bureau or Chamber of Commerce, state that fact at the bottom of the page. Include it on everything your public sees. This would include your business card, brochure and ads. It makes you a partner in a strong organization.

TELEPHONE

Answering machines are bad business. Hire a live person to answer the phone. Pay him or her well. The telephone is one of your most important tools. And, the person who answers the phone can mean the difference between success and failure.

Start out by hiring an answering service. Look for one that also takes credit card orders if you need them for your business.

Get a business listing. It costs a little more but you appear twice—in the white pages and in the *Yellow Pages*. You are in Directory Assistance, too. You do not need to include your address.

THE INTERNET

I advise you to get online as soon as possible, if you are not already there. The Internet is going to be your most important tool. Use it aggressively. It will make money for you and it will save you time.

It is almost impossible to run a business now without the Internet. Just think of it. Your customers are online as are your suppliers. You can find out about cutting-edge products and new trends online. You can run all your business communications through e-mail. *Not advisable! (Viruses)*

Information is power. And there is no greater

source of information than the Internet. All of the businesses in this guide rely on information to some degree.

Once you have more money, I recommend a second computer for use only with the Internet. I say this because of viruses and hackers. You want to protect the information on your hard drive at all costs.

FAX

Fax is one of the two cheapest means of communications. E-mail is the other. Use both as heavily and aggressively as you can.

Seven Keys to Success

Here are seven keys. They are easy to use and fit into any business. They sound simple but they are heavy movers and can help make your business a pleasure to run.

KEY #1: HIRING

Hire the smartest people you can find. Learn from them. They'll show you the ropes. They could carry you to the top.

Hire independent contractors to avoid paying benefits and taxes. This may cut about 30 percent off your payroll expenses.

Also, it's simpler to part company with an independent contractor if things don't work out.

Make sure the person satisfies the IRS's definition of an independent contractor. Otherwise, the IRS will call him or her an employee and charge you back taxes and penalties.

For part-time help on a business project, consider

going to a business school and requesting aid from graduate students. They are called interns. They are the brightest and the best and will often work hard to make your dream come true.

As a rule, you do not pay interns. They receive credit from the school for a work project.

KEY #2: BUSINESS CREDIT CARD

If you have trouble keeping track of what your business has spent, this card is for you. This card can make your accountant's work easier. It also shows the IRS that you are keeping your business funds separate and are not co-mingling them with your personal funds. *OK to mingle in LLC.*

At the end of the billing period, the card company will send a detailed list of everything you bought. You have only to hand it to your accountant.

There are other advantages to the business credit card. There is a float, or time period, when you still hold the money after you've paid. *? How*

The card can help control expenses. Make it a policy to pay for everything with it. To protect the card, authorize only one other person in your firm to use it. Otherwise, you may lose control over your company's cash flow.

KEY #3: TRADE ASSOCIATIONS

Join a trade association as soon as possible. You'll team up with experts in your field. They can show you new products, give advice and group insurance. They can bring you customers.

A good trade association can open doors for you. I've listed the best at the end of each business chapter.

Other Associations

The Chamber of Commerce and the Better Business Bureau are two of the most important groups to join. Through them you can meet other people in your area. Make contacts and form partnerships for advertising, shipping and supplies.

Some local merchants' associations are powerful. They might help with zoning, security and advertising.

National associations can give you a lot of help in Washington. Good ones are the National Association for the Self-Employed and the National Federation of Independent Business.

Membership in well-known associations is good marketing. It tells customers they can trust you.

KEY #4: BUY-SELL AGREEMENT

As soon as you find a lawyer, have him or her draw up a buy-sell agreement. It states what you want to happen to your business if you're unable to run it.

Family businesses are eaten up by lawyers and the government every day for lack of a buy-sell agreement. A business is like a child. It can live without you but it has to have someone to take care of it.

Also, banks ask to see a buy-sell agreement before granting a loan.

The agreement covers occurrences such as disability, divorce, retirement or death. It names the person you want to buy you out if you are in a partnership. It tells how the business should be valued. It also shows the value of your life insurance.

KEY #5: SUCCESSION PLAN

A succession plan is different from a buy-sell agreement. A buy-sell agreement transfers ownership of the business after you have left it. A succession plan is a transfer of ownership of the business while you are still around and may, in fact, still be working in it.

For sole proprietorships and closely-held family businesses, a succession plan is vital.

One in three businesses passes to the next generation.

Hire outside professionals to help select your successor. This removes you from the decision process. The successor might be a member of your family or an outsider. Setting up a succession plan in this way can defuse bitter family feuds over who gets the business.

Hire a professional to design a training program for your successor.

Gradually turn more of your work over to your successor. He or she should be the one working longer hours, not you.

KEY #6: DON'T SPEND MONEY

Here are two thoughts I keep in mind. They have helped many people and may help you, too:
- Don't buy anything you can't sell.
- If you do buy, buy the best.

Key #7: One Problem at a Time

What if things go wrong? You don't know how you're going to keep your business going another day, let alone another month. Here is a strategy that lifts the burden off your shoulders. It's a strategy that works if you give it a try.

Deal with *one* problem at a time. Take the most urgent and resolve it. That's all. Let the rest wait.

Leave the office. You've done your day's work.

It sounds simple. It is.

Mark Levine
877 381 3811

PART II
Which Business?

Business 1
Your Man in Rio

Did you know it's a mistake to give a clock as a gift in China? It brings bad luck. In France, if you are invited to dinner and bring a gift of flowers, choose them carefully. Chrysanthemums are for cemeteries, carnations are a bad luck flower and roses mean love . . . and the Socialists.

These small cultural differences can mean money in your bank account. Businesses of all sizes are marketing around the world. Many have manufacturing facilities abroad. But there's one thing that most of them lack—a knowledge of the country where they are doing business.

That's where you come in.

I called this chapter, "Your Man in Rio," because it relates to a firm I worked for in this field. Our man in Rio was a contract worker hired by the firm. In some cities it was a man—in others, a woman. And it wasn't only Rio. There was a contact person in Sao Paulo, Mexico City, Paris, Frankfurt, Milan, Hong Kong, Bangkok and other cities.

Let me show you exactly what my firm did. The strategy is simple. And, it's possible to make a lot of money.

THE BUSINESS

My firm started the business when trade barriers fell. Business people were flocking abroad. Some were opening offices in South America and in the Far East. Others were partnering with foreign firms in order to market their goods there locally. Manufacturers were dashing off to Recife in the east coast of Brazil and to the northern border towns in Mexico in search of cheap labor.

We first conducted a survey of several thousand American companies. We asked them what the biggest problems were that business people faced in foreign countries.

We asked these businesses how much they would pay per day for a service to help solve the problems they mentioned. And how much for an assistant to meet them in the foreign country and give them the help they needed.

There were other services we suggested such as finding suitable housing for business executives and their families. Supplying a car and driver. Locating schools for the children.

The businesses were willing to pay a substantial sum for such services. Surprisingly, it was the smaller and mid-size companies that offered to pay the most.

We used all the information to determine which services to offer and a fee schedule.

My firm focused on five cities: Bangkok, Hong Kong, Tokyo, Frankfurt and Paris. We contacted the trade mission from each country and received information about doing business there. The Department of Commerce, the International Chamber of Commerce and the Library of Congress gave enough information to build a small library.

This information went into reports that answered the questions of the businesses in the survey.

FINDING OUR MAN IN RIO

Finding somebody to be "our man in Rio" was the next step. We wanted a well-educated person in each city who would assist foreign business people. He or she would be fluent in English, possess a detailed knowledge of the city and be willing to work on a part-time basis.

We quickly located our main source—the university.

My firm interviewed graduate students from the school of business administration. They were energetic, knew their country well and were enthusiastic about meeting foreign business people.

We lined up students in each city. The students didn't need full-time jobs. They signed a contract with our firm and we agreed to pay them by the day. It was a perfect fit—for the students and for us.

We started out with ten students in each city so there would always be a back-up person. As business picked up, we hired more students.

While our clients were abroad, we contacted them

and asked if they were satisfied with the student assistant. If they were not satisfied, we got another assistant to take the place of the first.

The assistant filled out our time card. The client signed it and faxed it to us. We immediately credited the assistant's account.

If this sounds complicated, it's not. It is the easiest work in the world—and it's fun. You meet a lot of people. You can travel to fascinating places and make a lot of money at the same time.

It takes some organization to keep in touch with the student assistants in each city.

OUR SERVICE

Let me tell you how we promoted our service. Do you remember the survey we did? A large number of companies told us they might use our service. We concentrated on them and actually signed on quite a few as our first clients. Word of mouth brought us more clients.

We offered our service on a subscription basis. If a company was doing business in Bangkok, for instance, we sent it regular updates on Thailand. We supplied information on the business climate, political unrest, disease, weather and other foreign companies who were doing business there.

We also dealt with the problems the companies told us about on the survey. Some of those were:

- How do you get from the airport to the city?
- Is the faucet water safe to drink?
- Does the hotel give free bottled water?

Make the Money and Run

- Is there any special business etiquette? *Don't show your okge sole.*
- In doing business, is a gift expected? *No, but yes!*
- Where are there English-speaking lawyers? *ask them.*
- What are the names and numbers of English-speaking doctors and dentists? *Important!*
- Please give the correspondents of United States banks with their telephone numbers and hours.
- Where can one use an office with translators, secretarial service, computers and the Internet?

Our clients paid extra for the services of the assistant. If a client was not one of our subscribers, we charged double for the assistant service. *Gotcha' charge!*

Consulting was another service we offered. This usually involved teaching a short course on business etiquette for a particular country. This was held in the United States. Often, a firm would send a group of people to the course. Whenever we could, we hired a native of the foreign country as instructor.

We also carried out investigations for clients. We gathered up-to-the-minute public information about foreign companies.

We assessed the latest security and health risks in the country. *AIDS, malaria, Dengue fever, bullet holes!*

We had a visa service. Visas for Japan, for instance, fall into different categories. For a business trip you receive a short-stay commercial visa. You may enter Japan any time within four years and stay up to 180 days each time. The goods you bring in are duty-free up to a certain dollar amount.

Start your business with one foreign country. Perhaps you have traveled there or you come from

there. It should be open to trade. It should have other foreign firms doing business there.

When you feel more confident, add another country.

There is no scarcity of students to be assistants. Also, there are plenty of business people who need your service.

At times, a client may require more thorough investigative work. Hire a corporate P.I. firm that does international investigations. One such firm is Kroll Associates of New York.

FINDING CLIENTS

Now it's time to promote your service. You have to find clients. Here are some tips:

- One of the best places to find clients is at international trade shows. Hire a professional to design a brochure and business card. Hand out premiums to people. *[ad items]*

- Another effective way is direct mail. Rent a mailing list of small to mid-size firms that are likely to do business abroad. A mailing list broker will be able to find just the right list.

- Place a small classified ad in the trade journals of industries likely to do business abroad. This would include manufacturing, high-tech, defense and construction.

- Hire a public relations professional to make your name known to the business community.

Before your phone starts ringing off the hook, hire a live answering service. The service should be knowledgeable about your business and take callers' information so you can send them promotional material.

Follow up the promotional material with a telephone call to the company.

SIDE BUSINESSES

The related businesses are profitable and fun. There are many ways a person can assist people going abroad on business or relocating there

Here are a few:

- A consulting business is a natural outgrowth of "Your Man in Rio." Tailor your services to the type of client you have.
- Give courses in foreign business etiquette. You could handle the concerns of business travelers that I mentioned earlier. Make contacts for your clients abroad. Give them copies of English language newspapers and a directory of foreign firms or foreign residents in the country.

To find out about problem areas in the world, contact the International Air Transportation Associates (IATA).

- Country surveys are of prime interest to firms wishing to do business in a foreign country. This is an extremely profitable business. It's also a good business if you, yourself, want to travel abroad. *Do it? Maybe.* You would have to know exactly what your client wants to know and what his or her goals are. Hire a graduate student in statistics to make up a poll based on this information. Engage a polling firm in the foreign country to conduct the poll. Have the answers translated into English. The statistics student could analyze the results and give you a summary.

- What about a passport and visa service? This could save a business person time and provide a convenience. Saving a client time and making a task convenient for him or her are worth a great deal. Businesses pay dearly for such valuable service.

- Set up your own off-shore corporation in Ireland. This gives you an easy entry into the European market. Your office in Ireland could help clients who, themselves, want to do business in Europe. Also, having a European office greatly enhances your image as a solid company.

  Ireland permits one to set up an off-shore company in ten days. The cost is reasonable. The benefits are many. Also, the corporate tax is only ten percent.

The opportunities are plentiful. Start small and focus like a laser on one, small area.

What do you call reasonable?

Sweden, Spain, Germany,

corp tx 10%

Make the Money and Run 35

TIME ZONES AROUND THE WORLD

When it is 12:00 noon in New York ...
It is this time in ...

Santiago, Chile	1:00 PM
Sao Paulo, Brazil	2:00 PM
Reykjavik, Iceland	4:00 PM
London, England	5:00 PM
Zurich, Switzerland	6:00 PM
Cairo, Egypt	7:00 PM
Moscow, Russia	8:00 PM
Karachi, Pakistan	10:00 PM
Delhi, India	10:30 PM
Yangon, Myanmar (Rangoon, Burma)	11:30 PM
Bangkok, Thailand	12:00 MIDNIGHT
Kuala, Lumpur, Malaysia	12:30 AM (Next Day)
Singapore *No guns!*	12:30 AM (Next Day)
Beijing, China	1:00 AM (Next Day)
Hong Kong, China	1:00 AM (Next Day)
Tokyo, Japan	2:00 AM (Next Day)
Sydney, Australia	3:00 AM (Next Day)
Auckland, New Zealand	5:00 AM (Next Day)
Nome, Alaska	6:00 AM
Honolulu, Hawaii	7:00 AM
Los Angeles, California	9:00 AM
Denver, Colorado	10:00 AM
Mexico City, Mexico	11:00 AM
Washington, DC	12:00 NOON

WHAT TO DO

Conduct a survey of businesses
Focus on one or two foreign cities
Research those cities through U.S. Government sources
Form an S corporation or LLC
Obtain a corporate credit card
Obtain merchant status
Market your service as a subscription service
Line up assistants in the foreign cities
Set up a "Quick Corporation" in Ireland

RESOURCES

American Association of Exporters and Importers
11 W. 42nd Street
New York, NY 10036
(212) 944-10036

Morrison, Terry, Wayne A. Conaway, and George A. Bordon. *Kiss, Bow or Shake Hands: How to Do Business in Sixty Countries.* Holbrook, MA, Adams Media Corporation. 1994.

Small Business Exporters Association
1350 Beverly Rd., Ste. 617
McLean, VA 22101
(703) 761-4140

Business 2
Gift Albums

Get real!

How would you like to make a million dollars giving away free gifts? Valuable gifts that make everyone happy. And especially you—when you collect the money.

No one knows about this business. No one except Alex, an old family friend, who thought it up a few years ago. He kept it small—only himself—and quietly amassed his fortune.

So the field is fresh for you.

Let me tell you exactly how Alex got rich. You can copy what he did, step by step.

He came up with the idea of giving beautiful photo albums to parents of new babies. The albums would have expensive-looking leatherette covers. Each album would contain a note of congratulations from Alex's company.

Alex, himself, would deliver the albums to hospitals and make sure they reached the new mothers. He knew that the mothers and their families would be thrilled by the surprise gift.

How would Alex make money on these gifts? Here's how . . .

After he got the idea for the albums, he did a lot of research. Or, rather, he got professionals to do the research—for free.

ALEX'S PLAN

He went to the business school at the university. There, he presented his plan and was assigned a couple of graduate students in Business Administration. They would do the work and receive credit from the school for work experience. Alex wouldn't have to pay a dime.

The grad students made a list of businesses serving new parents and babies. There were shops that sold baby items and restaurants that welcomed parents who brought their infants with them.

They narrowed the list down to businesses with medium to large advertising budgets. They told Alex where each business advertised, how often they placed ads and how much they spent on advertising per quarter.

The students also estimated how many people responded to the ads. Most important, they worked out what the businesses received as a return on their advertising investment.

While the students were researching, Alex had 26 pages of ads printed. He copied past ads from the local businesses and had them reproduced in pastel colors. Each ad included a discount coupon and offered the customer a free gift for coming into the store.

In addition, Alex added important information on each page of ads. Items such as tips on baby care, recipes, most popular baby names with their origin and signs of the zodiac. In this way, mothers would keep the ad pages even after they used the coupons.

ADVERTISERS

Alex inserted the ad pages throughout a dozen or more sample albums. Then, he and his two graduate students along with a group of marketing students visited the businesses they had researched.

It took them only two weeks to sign on some 200 businesses. In the weeks that followed, Alex went around and was able to add more businesses. Some of them bought whole page ads. Others bought half a page or less.

So far, the businesses had committed several hundred thousand dollars.

Alex's big selling point to the business owners was this: He could guarantee them that their ad would run for an entire year. Plus that, at least 20,000 people would see the ad.

He knew that about 2000 babies were born in his area each year. Each one had about ten adult family members: two parents, four grandparents, two aunts and two uncles. Not to mention cousins and friends.

Another benefit Alex emphasized was that the new families had an income.

So, the business owners would be targeting a tight market with baby needs and money to spend. They wouldn't be wasting their advertising dollars on non-buyers. And since the parents received the album as a gift, they would be inclined to buy from the advertisers.

There was another incentive to advertise in the album. Alex told the owners they would probably receive a swift response to their ads. New families would start buying from them within a couple of months after they received the album. Response to ads on the Internet takes far longer. Even credit card companies wait as much as three years for a response to their ads.

The business owners understood the opportunity that Alex was offering them. They didn't need to add up the numbers. If only 25 percent of the new parents came into their stores, they could make a huge profit.

What really sold the business owners on the album, though, was the low cost. It averaged about $860 each. Why, they paid more that for only three weeks of ads in the newspaper.

MANUFACTURERS

All this time, Alex was researching album manufacturers at the library. He looked them up in the *Thomas Register* and telephoned each one.

The manufacturers sent him samples and price lists. He narrowed his list down to a couple of manufacturers, negotiated terms and chose the one he felt he could work with.

The manufacturer imprinted the cover with "Our Baby" in gold letters. He also printed the first page with spaces for the baby's name, date, time and place

of birth, weight, length and other data.
The album came in a white box with a pink or a blue ribbon. How about for twins? Triplets? More?

WHAT HAPPENED NEXT

The business owners signed Alex's contract and paid him one-half the ad cost up front. They paid the balance one week before the ad was printed.

Over the following years, Alex updated the album and added more advertisers. He visited the maternity wards regularly, kept up with the new births and made a lot of personal friends.

But, the baby album was not the only idea he pursued. Next came the wedding album. He followed the same procedure as with the baby album. Only this time he kept tract of marriages at city hall.

Weeks before the wedding he would contact the bride's family. They would be invited to drop by and pick up the free gift album. He selected about twenty merchants to distribute the albums in this way. They were happy to do this as it would bring potential buyers into their store.

The wedding album had just as much success as the baby album and some years, even surpassed it. Merchants were enthusiastic. Alex contacted about 300 advertisers. After a while, he didn't have to seek them out. They called him. Some even placed three and four ads in the same album.

He went on to try other items such as a senior prom album, baby's first Christmas or first Communion. But none of them made him the money that the new baby and the wedding albums did.

Do you see how easy this is? You can do the same thing.

There are more than 4 million babies born in the United States every year. If you get albums out to just one percent of the parents, you'll hand out 40,000 albums. Multiply that by the ten people who are going to see it and you have 400,000 potential shoppers. An ad in that album would sell itself.

What merchant wouldn't want to have exposure like that!

YOUR OWN BUSINESS

Follow Alex's steps. Don't change anything. As long as there are babies born and weddings held, you can make a fortune just the way he did.

Advertising is a major cost for any business. In the gift album business, you don't have to advertise your product. You give the albums away for free.

The only selling you have to do is to the business owners. Alex said that part was easy. When he showed the owners that 400,000 interested buyers would see their ad again and again, they jumped at it. Plus that, the price was right.

Require payment in full from the advertisers before the ad is printed. Once the ad is in the album, it's impossible to remove it if they don't pay.

There is an interesting side business. Produce a video cassette on "How to Care for Your Baby." Hire a professional studio to produce the film.

Ask shopkeepers to buy advertising segments in the film showing their product being used. The film would give directions to their store.

Just like the albums, the video cassettes would be given away as gifts. Discount coupons could also be included.

WHAT TO DO

Research the census data
Find prospective advertisers
Decide what kind of album you want
Form an S corporation or LLC
Obtain quotes from album manufacturers and suppliers
Get help from student interns
Produce a prototype album —— *?How?*
Have advertisers sign contract and pay you

RESOURCES

National Association of Manufacturers
1331 Pennsylvania Ave.
Ste. 1500 North Tower
Washington, DC 20004-1790
(202) 637-3000

Thomas Register of American Manufacturers
Thomas Publishing Company
5 Penn Plaza
New York, NY 10001

Business 3
Lighting Specialist

There is a quiet revolution going on. It's in the business of lighting. Anyone going into this business now, stands to make a lot of money.

Light, itself, has taken on a whole new meaning in the last few years. We are now looking at the effects of light on the human body. How it affects our mood and tells us when to sleep or wake up. Light is used as pure energy in lasers.

It is used in security to deter criminals. It is used in electronics to send messages and pictures. It makes plants grow indoors and provides warmth.

Now, let's see how it can make you money.

Here are three main types of lighting specialist:
- Lighting designer
- Interior lighting designer
- Architectural lighting designer

▶ As a *lighting designer*, you have the most leeway. You design lighting indoors and outdoors, for security, for commercial buildings, parking lots and gardens. You choose the type of light needed and the light level. You select fixtures and plan where to place them.

Three of the most popular indoor lighting fixtures are recessed lighting, the pendant light and directional lighting.

Recessed lighting is soft. A pendant light is focused on one area only. And directional lighting is dramatic. It can make a textured wall paper appear three-dimensional.

> ► As an *interior lighting designer*, your job is to match the light to the decor. The color of the light would be important. For instance, yellow incandescent light turns a red object orange. It makes a white object yellow.

You also have to consider people. Light that shines down from track lights or recessed ceiling lights makes people look older. It's best to use softfill light from wall sconces and torcheres.

> ► As an *architectural lighting designer*, you would cast certain parts of a building's exterior, a garden or square in dramatic light.

You would also work inside buildings or homes. Directional lighting would be used to highlight stairs, statues or decorative molding. The lighting should serve a function, as well, such as security or seeing your way through the dark.

Lighting is logical. You need no special skill. No license. All it requires is common sense. And an eye for trends.

HOW TO START YOUR OWN BUSINESS

Your first step is to do research. Study lights. Visit businesses, hospitals, restaurants and lighting stores. No one ever notices lights. We only see what the light shines on. But it is light that gives an object color and warmth and beauty. Stores are masters of lighting to lure the buyer.

Next, contact these trade associations for information:

>American Lighting Association
>Illuminating Engineering Society

Also, contact several lighting fixture supply houses in the *Thomas Register* in the library. Ask them for catalogues.

Finding clients should be easy. Ask the supply houses that you are going to do business with to help you. Have them set up a demonstration rack with lighting fixtures in a local hardware store to show to your clients.

Also, network with other businesses such as interior designers, hardware stores and business furniture stores. Let them refer their clients to you in exchange for your doing the same for them.

A profitable market is small companies. Many employees are working with computer screens. There is a lot of eyestrain. This is due to glare. Glare occurs when there is too much contrast between darkness and light. With a bright computer screen, it's important to keep the room filled with soft light from several directions.

Another problem is when ceiling lights cast hot spots on computer screens. This causes eye fatigue.

Turn off the ceiling lights and use uplights. They cast light upward toward the ceiling where it diffuses and gives off soft light.

On the job, listen to what the client wants. Write the client's wishes in your order book and have him or her make corrections and initial them. Get a blueprint of the room or outdoor space or draw your own plan. Include furniture or plants and other buildings.

Design the lighting on the blueprint and go to the client with your lighting design and contract. Everything should be approved and signed before you begin work. Require progress payments as each part of the job is finished.

How much should you charge? It depends on the locality in which you're working. Your price has to be in line with what your competitors are charging.

Use three different price scales. Charge the most for a big business, less for a small business and the least for a home.

For a business, have them sign a contract. Charge for the job as a *project*. For a residence, I recommend you charge *per room*. Many lighting specialists charge by the hour. But this makes the client push you to finish quickly. This leaves you no time to sell them extra fixtures or services.

There are three kinds of lighting. They are:

Ambient
Accent
Task

Ambient is a soft light that fills the room from several directions.

Accent is dramatic light that is directed on an object, such as a painting.

Task is light that is focused on a narrow field of work you are doing, such as reading or sewing.

There are two secrets to success. If you keep them in mind you will never fail.

- Focus the light where it is needed most. This is more complicated than it sounds. It means asking the person in charge what is expected of the light. What activities or objects need that light.
- All light should be balanced. This means filling a room with all three layers of lighting: Ambient, Accent and Task.

This prevents glare. Experts say that the difference between the brightest and the softest light in a room should be about three to one. And, never more than five to one.

There are many types of lighting you could concentrate on. Each has high enough profit potential for you to build your entire business around it. Here are some of them:

- Internal lighting for businesses and homes
- Indoor security lighting
- Outdoor security lighting
- Landscape lighting
- Tubular skylights (light pipes)
- Light around computer workstations and other worksites
- Full spectrum lights for homes, hospitals, retirement homes, schools and airports

I would like to say a word about tubular skylights: They bring sunlight into a dark house. They are easy to install. A dome on the roof collects the light and sends it down into the house through a tube with reflectors inside. Heat and UV rays are kept out. Sunshine is diffused throughout the room. This is a dynamic item and a profitable one.

Full spectrum lights are another exciting product. They provide natural sunlight without harmful UV rays. You can market these as simple bulbs or as lighted screens. Being exposed to this light can relieve insomnia and jet lag. It can make you more alert.

SIDE BUSINESS

- A good side business is light therapy. Open a salon equipped with full spectrum light booths. Light helps relieve depression. It would be similar to a tanning salon. Customers would occupy a "sun booth" fifteen to thirty minutes at a time. Contact the Society for Light Treatment and Biological Rhythms at the address at the end of this chapter.
- Selling unusual lights and fixtures can be profitable. Commercial clients such as hospitals, offices and plants buy in quantity. Sell to individuals through interior decorators, catalogues and cable television advertising.

WHAT TO DO

Form an S corporation or LLC

Obtain a business banking account

Have your attorney draw up a customer contract

Contact lighting fixture supply houses

Join two trade associations

Join the Better Business Bureau and Chamber of Commerce

Join a local merchants' association

RESOURCES

American Lighting Association (ALA)
World Trade Center, Ste. 10046
2050 Stemmons Hwy.
P.O. Box 42088
Dallas, TX 75342-0288
(214) 698-9898

Illuminating Engineering Society of North America
120 Wall Street, 17th Flr.
New York, NY 10005-4001
(212) 248-5000

Lighting Protection Institute
3335 N. Arlington Hts. Rd., Ste. E
Arlington Heights, IL 60004
(847) 577-7200

Society for Light Treatment and Biological Rhythms (SLTBR)
10200 West 44th Ave., Ste. 304
Wheat Ridge, CO 80033-2840

Make the Money and Run

United Lighting Protection Association (ULPA)
P.O. Box 22683
Lake Buena Vista, FL 32830-2683
(800) 668-UPLA

Business 4
Import-Export

If you have a variety store in your area, walk through the aisles. Pick up the merchandise and look where it's from. You'll probably find the rubber bands are from Thailand, the alarm clocks from Taiwan and the cigarette lighters from China. Even the clothing, pens, pencils and cooking pans are made abroad.

We make very few consumer goods now. I recently bought a Belgian waffle maker made in China. And a sweater from Mauritius. And I've just noticed I'm wearing Indonesian socks. All of which goes to say: We rely on imports. *Too much!*

Who imports these goods? Small companies and individuals, just like you and me.

IMPORTING

Importing is easier than you think. The reason why this is so is that you are here to receive the goods. You know they will not be held up in the customhouse or left to rot at dockside.

There are millions of goods you could import into the United States and make a fortune on. They don't have to be practical items, either. They could be pure fantasy like a new version of the Hula Hoop or a bottle of mountain air from the Himalayas.

I have a friend who imports handbags and belts from Pakistan. They are made of braided silk scarves. They're upscale and smart-looking. She is doing a booming business. And there is no competition.

As long as you have a buyer, you are in business. Where do you start?

Start with a customer. What kind of person do you want to sell to? Is it a man or a woman? A family person or a single? Young, middle-aged or older? Is he or she a traveler or a stay-at-home? What is his or her income? Get together with friends and work up a profile of the customer you want.

Once you know your customer, it's easier to find a product for him or her. Just look around and see what is selling. Scan the magazines at the check-out counter in the supermarket. They advertise fast-selling items.

Look for products at a trade show. Europe holds big trade shows a few times a year. Shows that specialize in collectibles, technology, inventions and household items are especially good hunting grounds.

Choose a number of products you think you can sell at home. But concentrate on selling only one product at a time.

Look up the code number of the products you want to import. Code numbers are in the Harmonized Tariff Schedule of the United States. It's available in most public libraries.

The next step is to find major buyers at home.

Choose buyers who are wholesalers. They sell products through manufacturers' reps, industrial distributors, department store chains, supermarket chains and mail order houses.

Wholesalers are the best. It is hard for you or me to sell directly to retail stores or small manufacturers. Wholesalers know the market inside and out. They can position your product to be a bestseller.

Visit as many as 100 wholesale buyers if you can.

Run a credit check on the serious ones. Look them up in Dun & Bradstreet.

Before showing them your product, package it attractively. Give it a fair retail price. When you show it to buyers, ask if they require any changes. Ask how many units they would buy and how much they would pay.

The next step is to contact the foreign supplier. This is easy. Look in the Compass Industrial Register. Also, every country has an Export Promotion Office here that you can contact.

You can find other information about suppliers in the Trade Channel newspaper from Holland which is available in libraries.

Dun & Bradstreet publishes an international directory called *Principal International Businesses*. It is a mine of information.

Contact the manufacturer directly. See if you can get exclusive rights to import their product into the United States.

Check out the manufacturer with the U.S. Department of Commerce.

The United States gives breaks on tariffs and

quotas to certain underdeveloped countries. You pay a lot less for goods from these countries. The Department of Commerce publishes the General System of Preference List that deals with this. It updates it daily.

There's another, wonderful break for importers. There are about 150 Foreign Trade Zones in the United States where you can warehouse your shipment without paying duty. Check with the Department of Commerce.

To pay foreign suppliers, you will probably give them an irrevocable letter of credit. This is a letter written by the importer's bank to the exporter. You, the importer, deposit payment for the goods in the bank. When the exporter proves that goods have been shipped, the importer's bank wires the payment to the exporter.

Here is the key question: Is it worth it to import the product?

Add up costs and subtract them from sales to your wholesaler. Your profit should be about 15 percent. That's $75,000 for every $500,000 shipment. Not bad if you can make eight or nine deals a year.

Remember, your profit depends entirely on the supplier's willingness to give you a price break. The supplier is the only one who will bend on price.

EXPORTING

If you see a product made at home that would work abroad, look into it right away. One hot item could set you up for life.

For instance, there is the famous case of the wind-up radios. They are a booming export to The Czech Republic and to parts of South America where electrical current is unreliable.

Other hot exports now are cable television equipment. Big money can be make by exporting hardware and software products to the Pacific Rim.

Investigate how much you may charge for your product abroad and how you will be allowed to advertise it. In France and other European countries there is a book-pricing law that forbids a larger discount than five percent for books. Television advertising of books and booksellers is not allowed.

The great advantage to exporting is that you have the Department of Commerce behind you. They will help with everything from choosing a product to making contacts abroad.

Another good source is the Export Opportunity Hotline operated by the Small Business Foundation of America (SBFA). Trade experts answer your questions and give advice.

Find a product in *The Journal of Commerce*. Each Friday morning it lists export opportunities. These are products for sale.

Attend trade shows in the United States. Look into sales of government surplus or companies that are liquidating their stock.

Visit the country you want to export to and get a feel for items that could be sold there profitably. The Department of Commerce can give you contacts and help.

There is a lot of profit to be made in exporting disposable medical supplies to Russia and to many other parts of the world.

You could find a high-priced item that already has a steady demand such as art. One businessman I know, brings American paintings to London and British paintings to America. He travels with the paintings. He makes a six-figure income and deals with a small group of people he knows well.

To find a buyer abroad, go to trade shows abroad. Make arrangements ahead of time so you can rent a booth. Have samples of the product to give out along with your card and brochure.

Also, have the United States International Chamber of Commerce put you in touch with business brokers. A good broker can smooth the way for you to sell your product abroad.

It's helpful to have demographic information about the country to which you are exporting. Other aids are a business address, bank account, office and telephone number in that country. The Department of Commerce can help. Contact their Center for International Research in Washington, DC.

Contact the Small Business Administration's Office of International Trade. Ask for free counseling, training and legal help.

You might hire a foreign intermediary company to represent you in that country. Choose carefully, however. In France, for instance, you may be sued if you fire the intermediary company that represents you.

Consider opening an offshore company in Ireland. This would give you a presence in the European Union. Also, corporate taxes in Ireland are very low and expenses are also low.

Ireland has three ways of incorporating your off-

Make the Money and Run 59

shore company:
- Quick Incorporation takes only ten days.
- Tailor-made Incorporation takes six to eight weeks.
- Shelf Company, in which you purchase an existing corporation that is not being used. It can be used immediately.

Fees are reasonable and you can set up an offshore company through a law firm in the United States.

Here are two short-cuts to exporting that reduce a lot of risk:

♦ Network. Partner with other exporters who have a market presence in the country you've chosen. Select exporters who are not competitors. You would use their export channels in return for sharing costs.

♦ Hire an export management company to find buyers for your goods abroad. This may be a United States company that acts as an intermediary to distribute your product abroad.

In importing as well as exporting, professionals move your product. These professionals are freight forwarders, customs brokers and import agents.

Fees to pay include import duties, freight and insurance.

Work with a large international bank such as Citibank.

To get acquainted with import-export documents, send away for a catalogue. Call UNZ & Company at (800) 631-3098.

If you don't want to deal with shipping and customs yourself, there are two professionals who can do it for you. They are the *freight forwarder* and the *overnight courier service*. They handle domestic and foreign customs, regulations, shipping, storage and insurance.

Use a freight forwarder for a large, bulky shipment such as 1000 rolled-up carpets. Use an overnight courier service for small, light-weight items, such as 1000 pen and pencil sets.

SIDE BUSINESSES

Here are a few of many, profitable side businesses:

- Form your own export management company and represent United States manufacturers. Your job would be to find foreign buyers for their goods. For this, you would earn a commission.
- Become an international trade consultant. You can obtain almost all the information and training you need free of charge from the Department of Commerce and the Office of International Trade at the Small Business Administration.
- A 900 # telephone trade updates service can be a lucrative business. Give daily updates on the Department of Commerce's General System of Preference List. The information on the List changes daily, without warning. Include news from the World Trade Organization such as

tariff reductions and settled disputes.
- An international protection service for the business traveler is a powerful money-maker. Terrorism and extortion are growing apace with global trade. Business people want to feel safe. A protection service should concentrate on two areas:

   Protecting the business person while abroad

   Teaching him or her self protection

   Subcontract security firms to provide the training and the protection.

WHAT TO DO

Form an S corporation or LLC
Get a business address
Open a corporate bank account
Obtain merchant status —— *how?*
Join a trade association of importers/exporters
Obtain information from the Department of Commerce
Read *The Journal of Commerce* and trade publications
Obtain a local license if necessary
Obtain a tax identification number
Contact the Export-Import Bank about exporting
Attend trade shows

RESOURCES

American Association of Exporters and Importers
11 W. 42nd Street
New York, NY 10036
(212) 944-10036

Export-Import Bank of the United States
(800) 424-5201

Export Opportunity Hotline
Small Business Foundation of America (SBFA)
811 Vermont Ave. NW
Washington, DC 20004
(202) 565-3946

Foreign Trade Association
Weyerstrasse 2
D-5000 Cologne 1
Germany

Ireland Chamber of Commerce in the U.S., Inc.
1305 Post Road
Fairfield, CT 06430
(203) 255-4774

Small Business Administration
Office of International Trade
(202) 205-6720

Small Business Exporters Association
1350 Beverly Rd., Ste. 617
McLean, VA 22101
(703) 761-4140

U.S. Department of Commerce
Ste. 1500, North Lobby
1331 Pennsylvania Avenue
Washington, DC 20004-1703

Compass Industrial Register

The Journal of Commerce

Business 5
Newsletter

Have you heard of *The Tightwad Gazette*? It was a newsletter started by Jim and Amy Dacyczyn. It showed people how to save money by using everyday objects such as tin cans or empty milk cartons in a variety of ways. It was a great idea.

The most interesting thing about it, however, is the money it brought in. The owners started on a shoestring and within just one year made $750,000!

You can do it, too.

And, even if you don't do as well as the Dacyczyns, you could surely get 2000 subscribers, charge a modest $50 an issue and gross $100,000 a year. That's not bad for the first year or two. You may be able to double or triple that amount over the next few years. And, if you add an extra product or service, it could boost your bottom line.

FINDING A TOPIC

First of all, decide what to write about. All newsletters focus on a single topic. *The Tightwad Gazette* was about saving money.

Write about what you already know. Or choose a topic that you can become an expert in. Popular subjects are weight-loss, making money in a particular business, stocks, nutrition, collectibles, organic gardening and making and selling crafts.

With the popularity of online auctions, collectibles are a hot topic.

Look at the competition. Are there other newsletters on your topic? Choose a popular subject where there is a lot of competition. It tells you there's interest in it. It's better to be in a crowded field than alone with a product no one wants.

You can always find an angle to make your newsletter unique such as a telephone hotline, a Web site, discount coupons or a fax-on-demand service.

Next, determine who your customers will be. And how much to charge. An easy way to do this is to answer these questions:

Who would read my newsletter?
How much money do they make?
How much money would they pay for a newsletter?
Do they buy through the mail?
What kind of information do they want?
What benefit does my newsletter give them?
Who are my competitors?
How much do they charge?

Choose a name for your newsletter that describes it and is easy to remember. *The Tightwad Gazette* is a perfect example of a first-rate name.

WRITING THE NEWSLETTER

Your aim is to give your subscribers specific information fast. They don't have time to find it on their own. Your subscribers rely on you as an expert. The information you give them in capsule form will help them make decisions.

You should also give them your opinion. Subscribers want you to take a stand. Make predictions.

Never include ads. Subscribers are paying you a lot of money and do not want to read ads. Also, having ads may give the impression you are biased.

Where do you find information to write about?

Online databases is an excellent way. Contact the Gale Directory of Databases and ask them to send you a catalogue.

Newsletters, magazines, newspapers and books are good sources. Subscribe to a clipping service. Give them subjects and they will sift through publications and send the information to you.

Write to companies and ask to be placed on their press list. This is easy to do. They will send you regular updates about them and their products.

Survey your subscribers for ideas and leads. They are often experts in the field. Some will write articles for you.

PRINTING THE NEWSLETTER

Print your newsletter inexpensively. People are buying the information it contains, not the way it looks. You can run it off on a computer printer and have as many copies made as you need. Or, bring it to Kinko's to make copies.

It can be four, eight or twelve pages or more. More pages does not mean you can charge more.

Use words and not pictures. Pictures do not sell well unless they show how to do a particular thing.

Use white paper with black ink. Divide pages into two or three columns. People are used to reading newspaper columns.

On the masthead, at the top of the first page, place:

- Newsletter title
- Your name, address and telephone number
- Date and issue number

At the bottom of the first page, include:

- Copyright notice
- Retail subscription price
- Telephone number
- Fax number and e-mail address

Put a disclaimer at the bottom of the first or second page.

Decide how often your newsletter will appear. Rather than giving a specific publication date, you might state there are nine issues a year. That way, you avoid being locked into a deadline.

GETTING SUBSCRIBERS

The best way of getting subscribers is by direct mail. This means renting lists of people most likely to subscribe to your newsletter. Mail out sales letters to these people. They subscribe, sending either a check with the order form or telephoning their subscription and paying with a credit card. *PayPal?*

Rent the best lists. The best are newsletter subscriber files. These are people who already subscribe to other newsletters. A newsletter reader often subscribes to two more newsletters. Lists of magazine and newspaper subscribers are also good but not as good.

How do you find newsletter subscriber files?

The job is made easy if you use a list broker. He or she is an expert in lists and can be found in *SRDS* (*Standard Rate and Data Service, Inc.*). This reference book is in most libraries.

Your sales letter and order card make up 40 percent of your success in gaining a subscriber. Hire a professional copywriter to write them. It's worth every penny. You can't leave something that important to chance.

Tips to help you gain subscribers:
- Keep your offer simple
- Offer a 100 percent money back guarantee
- Offer a free bonus such as a report or a calculator

Use the "Bill me later" technique in your offer. Wording to use is "Send no money now. We will bill you later." This is a phenomenal selling strategy. It means, "we trust you." It has powerful appeal and will bring you many subscribers.

Your profits come from renewals. They are inexpensive. Start sending the renewal offer after two or three issues. Show the benefits of continuing the subscription and include another free bonus. Set a price deadline. Beyond a specific date, the subscription price will rise by 50 percent, for example.

SIDE BUSINESSES

There are some interesting side businesses you can start. One of them is a pay-per-call telephone number. The caller is charged per minute. Offer updates on whatever your newsletter is about.

- Audio tapes and videos sell well. If you can tie them into the information in your newsletter, you will see profits soar.

- Seminars are another high-profit sideline. Again, stick to the theme of your newsletter. Many newsletter writers hold week-long seminars on cruises or in major cities and invite guest speakers. You can charge a high price. Make videos of the events and sell them.

- Become a consultant. You can do this by telephone. Even if it's long distance. For instance, if your newsletter deals with art appraisals, have a client call your toll-free number. He or she would describe the piece and pay with a credit card. Do the research and call the person back with your appraisal. Send him or her a hard copy of it by mail, also.

WHAT TO DO

Choose a popular topic for your newsletter
Make a profile of prospective subscribers
Develop an angle to make your newsletter stand out
Print your newsletter inexpensively
Decide if you want online subscribers
Decide if you want a hotline
Set a subscription price
Advertise by direct mail

RESOURCES

Beach, Mark. *Editing Your Newsletter* Portland, OR, Coast to Coast Books, 1988

Hudson's Subscription Newsletter Directory
The Newsletter Clearinghouse
P.O. Box 311
44 West Market Street
Rhinebeck, NY 12572-1403
(914) 876-2081

Newsletter & Electronic Publishers Association
1501 Wilson Blvd., Ste. 509
Arlington, VA 22209-2403
(703) 527-2333

Oxbridge Directory of Newsletters
Oxbridge Communications, Inc.
150 Fifth Avenue #302
New York, NY 10011-4311
(800) 955-0231

70 Make the Money and Run

SRDS (Standard Rate and Data Service, Inc.)
1700 Higgins Rd.
Des Plaines, IL 60018
(800) 851-7737

Business 6
Mail Order

Golden-amber brandy from France . . . gargoyles from Italy . . . blue sapphires from Sri Lanka . . . hand-painted tiles from Turkey . . . silver bells from Nepal . . .

This sounds like an exotic bazaar. Actually, they are a few of the millions of items you can sell in your mail order catalogue.

Mail order is the king of businesses. Did you know that twice as much merchandise is sold by mail order as by retail stores? It is a $400 billion industry.

Mail order has made millions for many people. It can do the same for you.

Have you seen Lillian Vernon catalogues? This giant of the mail order industry started out with just two items—a handbag and a belt. They were personalized with the customer's initials. Her first, small ad appeared in a 1951 issue of Seventeen magazine.

Lillian Vernon started her business from the kitchen table as a young woman. Today, the Lillian Vernon Corporation brings in several hundred million dollars a year.

START YOUR OWN BUSINESS

Set up your business as an S corporation or as a limited liability company. LLC

Rent a large box at a commercial mail box service.

Decide who your customers will be. Will you sell to businesses or individuals? Will they be golfers? Travelers? Gardeners?

Next, find three products that will sell like hotcakes. Stick to related products. For instance, if you deal in dolls, your choice of products could include dolls' clothes or doll houses. In security products, you might carry sprays, locks and alarms.

Look up suppliers in the *Thomas Register* in the library. Get in touch with them.

If you fill the orders yourself, choose products that are small and light weight. Sell items that don't break or spoil easily.

If you dropship, you have less work. In dropshipping, you receive the order and payment. You simply forward the order, your mailing label and the supplier's portion of the payment along with postage to the supplier. The supplier ships the item as if it came directly from you.

Feature only one product in your ads. When orders come in, tuck some sales literature about your other products in the package. Be sure to include an order form and a return self-addressed envelope.

If you are dropshipping, have the supplier do this.

Print up a catalogue. People like looking through catalogues in their slippers and looking at pictures of inlaid wood from Damascus or sherpa parkas from Nepal. They will read every word you write.

FINDING CUSTOMERS

Here are the ways mail order specialists catch the customer's eye:

- **Two-step advertising.** Place a small ad in a magazine and people will write for more information. Reply with a sales letter. Those interested will then send you an order. It is especially effective with higher priced items over $10.
- **Directly from the advertisement.** Your ad contains all the information, often including an order form. The customer sends in the order directly from the ad. This is usually used for items under $10.
- **Direct mail.** Mail your sales literature to names on a list. You may rent the list from others or use your in-house list of customers.
- **Direct selling salespeople.** You recruit salespeople who are paid according to the amount they sell. You may guarantee a minimum income the first year as an incentive.

I've had the best results with the two-step advertising and selling directly from the ad.

In the two-step ad, a top-notch sales letter is vital. Read sales letters you get in the mail. Study the good ones. They focus on one or two benefits. The writer talks to you as if you are an old friend.

Selling directly from the ad requires a professionally written ad. Focus on *one* benefit only.

There has been a lot written about what makes people buy. Psychologists tell us there are certain powerful words that grab the reader's attention. Put them in your sales letter or ad. Here are a few:

Free	Amazing	How to	New	Now
At last	Secret	Easy	Miracle	Success

THE BEST PRODUCTS

What are the best products to sell?
The following are good ones:

- Vitamins. There is a health craze going on around the world. People are already sold on the miracle of vitamins and food supplements. That makes your job easier.

    You can sell either generic vitamins or brand names. Either way, you can make a good profit. Be sure to carry product liability insurance. Also, use disclaimers telling customers that you do not guarantee a medical improvement or a cure.

- Kitchen items. People must eat and most have kitchens. They spend millions of dollars on bread machines, pasta machines, graters, food processors, spatulas and wooden spoons.

- Jewelry. Best sellers, in order of popularity, are earrings, pins, brooches, bracelets, rings, charms, pendants, necklaces, watches, tie tacs, clasps and cufflinks.

- Collectibles. Collectibles are red-hot now. Perhaps this is due to online auction houses. Almost anything you find in your attic may be snapped up online. The idea is to find a popular product or an angle. The product might be a good-luck charm. As for an angle, a friend of mine has a good one. He sells Hollywood memorabilia. It started as a hobby and has proven to be a gold mine. You can do the same thing. There's room for everybody.

How should you price items?

If the item costs you about .50, charge $1. If it costs you $1, charge $2.95, $2.98 or $2.99. Avoid charging increments of .50, such as $2.50, $3.50 and so on.

For items over $1, mark your item up at least three times. If that price seems too outrageous, choose another product.

With collectibles, paintings and antiques, there is a lot of room for mark-up.

Catalogues are a good way to market your product. Place your items in someone else's catalogue. There are companies searching for people who will advertise in their catalogue.

For a fee of a few thousand dollars, some smaller catalogue companies will carry your item in nine or ten different catalogues. The catalogue company will fill the order and you may receive as much as 70 percent of the retail price. For bigger catalogues with best selling items, you probably will receive far less but you may sell more of your product.

If you mail your own catalogue, you can hire a fulfillment center to fill your orders. The center receives the order and ships the item. It also keeps track of your inventory and tells you which items sell the best. The fulfillment center may take as much as 30 percent of the retail price of the product plus postage.

If you want to make more money in mail order, sell overseas and in Mexico and Canada. American goods are known to be of high quality. Many locals prefer them to their own, local products.

Your sales literature should be translated into the language of the country where you're selling.

One man I know sells fruit drinks to Mexico. He has a big, thriving market. He maintains that the *water* in his drinks has made him a success. The drinking water in Mexico is generally not safe so the people have more faith in *his* drinks. Clean water would sell well anywhere in the world.

Also, the more related products you offer, the more profit you make. Does your product lead to another product you can offer? If you sell lamps, for example, you could offer mini-lights that hook onto your keys or strobe lights for joggers.

SIDE BUSINESSES

You can create many side businesses. Here are three:

- **Consulting**. Once you have experience running a mail order operation, you could advise other marketers at a high fee.
- **Catalogue Design**. If you can design a catalogue for others, you could make enough money to make that your main business.
- **Trade Shows**. There is a blockbuster mail order show held each year. But, there is room for others. You could organize your own trade show and make a fortune.

WHAT TO DO

Form an S corporation or LLC
Decide whom to sell to
Research different products
Contact suppliers for samples
Select three products
Slowly expand your catalogue
Concentrate on your best-selling items

RESOURCES

Ad Mail Marketing Association
1901 N. Ft. Myer Drive, Ste. 401
Alexandria, VA 22209-1609
(703) 524-0096

American Marketing Association
311 S. Wacker Dr., Ste. 5800
Chicago, IL 60606
(800) 262-1150

Direct Marketing Association
1120 Avenue of the Americas.
New York, NY 10036-8096
(212) 768-7277

Hicks, Tyler. *Mail Order Success Secrets.*
Rocklin, CA, Prima Communications, Inc., 1998.

Lewis, Herschell G. *More Than You Ever Wanted To Know About Mail Order Advertising.*
New York, Prentice-Hall, 1983.

Mail Order Product Guide
B. Klein Publications
P.O. Box 6578
Delray Beach, FL 33482
(561) 496-3316

The National Directory of Mailing Lists
Oxbridge Communications, Inc.
150 Fifth Ave., Suite 302
New York, NY 10011-4311
(800) 955-0231

National Mail Order Association
2807 Polk St., NE
Minneapolis, MN 55418-2954
(612) 788-1673

Powers, Melvin. *How to Get Rich in Mail Order.*
North Hollywood, CA, Wilshire Books, 1980.

Business 7
Dating Service

If there are any singles bars in your area, stroll by them some evening after eight o'clock. You'll probably see a crush of people inside and others, outside, pressing to get in. Friday night is when they're particularly crammed. Saturday nights, too.

This spells opportunity for you.

Tens of millions of people are looking for a mate. The biggest market is between the ages of 28 and 45. A lot of people have put off marriage for a career. Many are divorced. Others never married.

The dating service is tremendously profitable. That's why bars, restaurants, sports clubs and some church groups are involved in it.

Your dating service could help a small percentage of these people. I say *small* percentage because it's important to specialize in a niche market.

A small group of people with something in common. That is how a person can make the most money.

FIND A NICHE

There's a bar in my area that caters to singles. The proprietor understands niche marketing. He's after the well-heeled, "forty-something" customer.

He promotes the place as the "Captain's Club." And it is a sort of club. There's a high cover charge and the same core group of people are there every night. The proprietor knows them personally. Some of those who meet at his club marry each other.

New people come in every night by invitation only. About half become members. The proprietor sends invitations to people he selects off a list.

Finding a niche means serving a narrow group of clients.

Attract upscale customers so you can charge high fees. Once your business takes off, open offices in cities around the world.

Focus on the business community. If you have a large Hispanic population, narrow it down to Hispanic business singles.

Other niches:
- Animal lovers
- Single parents
- Around the world travelers
- Scientists

Listen to this success story:

"It's Just Lunch," a dating service headquartered in Chicago, dealt only in business people. According to the last description I read, customers paid $675 for a six-month membership plus eight dates. Annual membership cost $975 with a minimum of fifteen dates. Founder Andrea McGinty started her company on just $6000. Annual revenues were upward of $3 million. They had offices around the country.

You have everything it takes to do the same thing.

Advertising is not expensive. Rely on word of mouth. When you do advertise, limit it to your target market. That saves you from squandering your money on markets that have no interest for you.

Charge a registration fee. Make it $1000 or more. This defines you as a high class service. It attracts the affluent and helps keep away weirdos. The registration fee might also cover the first date. After that, you could charge $300 to $500 for each introduction.

BACKGROUND CHECK

Each client should sign a contract drafted by your attorney outlining your services and policies. Before accepting a client, screen him or her. You do not have to accept everyone. In fact, it's better that you choose your clients carefully and keep them within the market you are targeting.

To protect your clients, do a background check. There are many companies that do this. Contact one and have them run a check for a police record and other personal data. Ask the client for written permission to do the background check.

Sign a contract with the company that does the search. Most require reasonable annual and monthly maintenance fees. In addition, there is a fee for each search.

CUSTOMIZE

Customize your dating service. For instance, you might match clients using astrology. Astrology matchmaking is all the rage, particularly in Japan.

One way of customizing your service is by being exclusive.

At last account, Christine O'Keefe of Beverly Hills, California, charged a minimum fee of $5000. She would introduce a client to up to twelve candidates.

Perfect Match, a dating service in Los Angeles, was, as I heard, phenomenally high-tone. They matched up the very rich - for a minimum fee of $100,000.

SET UP YOUR OWN BUSINESS

How do you set up your own dating service? Follow these steps:

- Check demographics for singles in your area.
- Research the competition and answer these questions:

    How many other dating services are there?

    How are they doing?

    Which particular clientele do they specialize in?

    What do they offer?

    How much do they charge?

    Once you know the answers, copy exactly what the competition is doing and add something

extra. You will stand out from the others. Promote this one valuable extra service the others don't offer. *What? Limo?*
- Next, open your office in an upscale neighborhood. Rent quality furnishings, the latest video equipment and lighting. Buy a computer.

Resort areas, by the way, are tops for dating services. Many people go on vacation to look for a mate.

- Have your lawyer draw up a client registration and contract.
- Have the client fill out a standard questionnaire. This could include age, sex, education, marital status and occupation. And the usual physical characteristics such as height, weight and color of eyes and hair.

Let the client specify what he or she is looking for in a mate. These might include physical characteristics, education, financial status and position in society.

- Videotape the client for two to three minutes. This could take place while you are having a friendly chat with him or her.
- Attract clients with wine and cheese parties. Everybody likes them and you can hold them in an art gallery or on a yacht.
- Seek free publicity. Be a guest on radio and television talk shows. Send news releases to the local media. Have someone write an article about you and your service.
- Use paid advertising including a listing in the *Yellow Pages*, small magazine ads and a Web

site. One of the best ads is topping. Your ad appears on top of taxis cabs.

There will always be plenty of singles. Your reputation is the secret to success. Once people trust you, you'll know the time has come for you to open offices all over the country - and soon, all over the world.

SIDE BUSINESSES

There are some money-making side businesses where you can have a bit of fun, too.

- **Mail Order.** Your product would be a newsletter with descriptions of your members. Have them sign a written agreement to this. The newsletter could be mailed to subscribers all over the world. The subscription fee would be very high, of course, to keep it out of the hands of voyeurs and kooks. Offer audio cassettes for sale with the members own voices.
- **Mail Order Catalogue.** This would be a good way to market upscale products aimed at singles. Some of the items might be singles' tours or parties. Sports clothes for affluent singles. Ski trips and sailing classes would appeal to many singles.
- **Image Consulting Service.** Make videos of clients to help them achieve a successful image for television interviews or business presentations. Advise them about clothing, hair and grooming. Hire an acting coach to give them speech and acting lessons.

- **Bride and Groom Service.** Here is a side business that I saw in Japan. It is a bride and groom make-over service. Four days before the wedding, the bride and groom are trimmed, tucked and beautified. Clothes are selected. The service takes care of the wedding guests, too. All the wedding preparations and the honeymoon are arranged by the service as well.

WHAT TO DO

Research census data on singles in your area

Study the competition

Find a niche

Survey 50 to 60 singles in your niche market to test interest

Form an S corporation or LLC

Buy liability and other insurance

Hire an attorney

Rent an office in an upscale area

Rent lights and video equipment

Advertise

RESOURCES

Metro Creative Graphics, Inc.
33 W. 34th St.
New York, NY 10001
(212) 947-5100
(News release service)

Business 8
Pet Boarding

If you love animals, here's a business that is tailor-made for you. Pet boarding can add passion and happiness to your life. It can also make you rich. The market is wide open. This business is still in its infancy.

How big is the market? Consider this - approximately 33 million Americans own pets. And 99 percent of them have not boarded their pets or used a pet sitting service, yet. Many are afraid to leave their pets in the care of a service. They fear the animal may be mistreated.

Once they learn that a pet-friendly service such as yours exists, they'll come in droves.

An additional attraction to pet boarding are the side businesses you can easily take on. They could add several hundred thousand dollars to your bottom line. We'll come to them, later.

HOW TO OPEN YOUR BUSINESS

Start your business by contacting the American Boarding Kennels Association. Their address is at the end of this chapter. They offer a starter kit, insurance, special training and legal help.

Next, research your location. There are strict zoning laws in many areas. Ask your local city hall about zoning.

What facilities do you have? Cats and dogs need dry, clean indoor living areas that are separate from your own living quarters. Dogs, particularly, need space.

Several buildings are needed for cats and dogs. Sick animals should be kept in a separate facility from healthy ones. Mange and ringworm spread quickly and can infect all your animals.

Now it's time to decide who your clients will be. Do you want cat owners? Dog Owners? Horse owners? Or all three? Maybe you have room for exotic animals and birds?

If you board reptiles, be sure they do not come into contact with other animals.

If you board dogs and cats, the buildings where they live should be far apart. Unneutered males and females must be kept in separately enclosed areas. All quarters should be clean, light, airy and free of odors.

Dogs need a run where they can exercise. They also need an outdoor area where they can be walked regularly and where they can take care of their needs.

Cats need open space indoors. Kitty litter belongs far away from where they eat. Granular litter is usually better than clumping.

Learn about common diseases. To protect the other boarders, you may require that an animal be immunized before you board it.

Leading dog illnesses are heart worm, distemper and rabies.

Among cats, the leading disease is feline leukemia. It is untreatable and ends in death. Another disease is feline immunodeficiency virus. It has nothing to do with human HIV. A cat cannot infect a human with this disease.

The amount you charge depends entirely on your location. A median price might be $150 per month for a dog and $75 for a cat. In a resort area, this would be more. For shorter periods, such as a week or a few days, the cost would be higher.

The client would pay extra for grooming and special food as well as teeth and ear cleaning.

Boarding horses is a lot of fun. I grew up with our own horses and we boarded other peoples. Each animal needs a dry, clean stall. A high-quality mixture of oats, mash and vitamins twice a day. Enough hay to last all day and a salt lick are also a necessity.

How much do you charge? Again, it depends on where you live. Rates for horse boarding vary from $50 to $500 a month, depending on location.

In addition to daily grooming, the horse needs a pasture to graze in and his or her stall cleaned twice a day. Horses' hooves need cleaning daily and should be trimmed every seven to ten days.

If this seems like a lot of work, it is. But it is joyful work. Still, I urge you to hire a few hands if you have a lot of animals. Most important - your helpers must be kind to animals. Hire them on a contract basis for a trial period of six months.

Contract with a couple of local veterinarians. Agree to use them exclusively. Your clients will be paying the bill and a low-cost vet service may induce them to board their pets with you.

Boarding horses is very profitable. Many horse owners board out their animals for an entire season - usually the winter. If they want their horses ridden two or three times a week, they should pay an extra fee.

I recommend you ask for the entire boarding cost of any animal up front. Also, demand a deposit to cover potential veterinarian fees. This is to ensure that you get paid. Most people will gladly pay to have their pet in good hands.

For extra services such as bathing and grooming, giving medicines or special feeding routines, charge an extra fee. Running the animal to the vet would be a special charge.

Have clients sign a contract. Do not accept responsibility if a pet dies, falls ill or is hurt in your facility. You also should carry sufficient liability insurance and an umbrella policy. These are not expensive.

FINDING CUSTOMERS

The next question is: how do you reach your buyers? The best way is through veterinarians in the area. Pay them a few dollars for every pet owner they refer to you. Do the same with dog grooming salons, pet shops and travel agencies. Get listed on local area *Yellow Pages* on the Internet.

Send news releases to the local media. Post a notice of your new service on bulletin boards in the library and supermarkets. Place classified ads in magazines that cat, dog and horse owners read. Local shopkeepers will let you put a small notice about your business in their windows for a few dollars.

Show that you are a professional by joining a trade association. Also, join the Better Business Bureau and the Chamber of Commerce. Buy professional business cards and letterhead.

SIDE BUSINESSES

Now for those profitable side businesses I mentioned earlier. They are so good I cannot wait to tell you about them.

- The first is a pet cemetery. Here again, zoning is the main question. If you're not allowed to build a cemetery on your property, you can buy a small lot further in the country, cheaply.

    Pet funerals are big business. Many owners want their dead pets cremated. Others want the skin preserved by a taxidermist or they want the remains freeze dried. If you go into the pet funeral business you could contract out this work to experts and receive a commission. The same is true for granite grave markers.

- You may also sell medical and death insurance for pets.
- Consider providing a counseling service for grieving owners whose pets have died. In this business, you are known as a "bereavement fa-

cilitator." If this sounds far-fetched, it is not. The demand for such services is wide-spread and goes unmet. You would work with the owners through their stages of grief. You might lead successful support groups. Also, you might be called upon to replace the pet with another.

Cloning a pet is being researched at Lazaron Bio Technologies LLC. Check "Resources" for their address.

- Animal day care centers are all the rage now in major cities. They are set up much the same as child day care. Cameras are placed throughout the center to enable the pet owner to view his or her pet on the Internet.

  Knowing first aid for animals could be a highlight of your business. Pet Tech, Inc. offers first aid courses. Check "Resources" for their address.

- Another sideline is pet sitting. This business can bring in over $400,000 a year, according to trade association, Pet Sitters International. In this business, you and your employees will be entering people's homes. You and they will have to be bonded and you should carry liability insurance.

- Yet another profitable line is selling personalized T-shirts, tote bags, mugs, stickers, postcards and other items. You could sell these items by catalogue or by e-commerce over the Internet. The customer would send in a photo of his or her pet with an order. A specialty printer or photographer could transfer the photo onto the item. Request payment with the order.

Include in your catalogue the new K-Kollar, jewelry decorated with animals, travel carriers, odor eliminators, scratching posts and beds. Offer grooming kits for horses.

WHAT TO DO

Contact the American Boarding Kennels Association
Attend Pet Services Annual Convention and Trade Show
Check local zoning laws
Find out if you need a local license
Decide which animals to board
Form an S corporation or LLC
Join two professional associations
Obtain liability insurance and bonding, if necessary
Market your business
Hire a telephone answering service
Contact local veterinarians
Find suppliers of animal food and grooming products

RESOURCES

American Boarding Kennels Association
1002 East Pikes Peak Ave.
Colorado Springs, CO 80909
(719) 591-1113

American Grooming Shop Association
1002 East Pikes Peak Ave.
Colorado Springs, CO 80909
(719) 591-1113

American Pet Boarding Association
2206 N. Pet Lane
Prairie View, IL 60069
(847) 634-9447

International Association of Pet Cemeteries (IAPC)
P.O. Box 163
5055 Rte. 11
Ellenburg Depot, NY 12935
(518) 594-3000

Lazaron Bio Technologies LLC
Louisiana Business & Technology Center
Baton Rouge, Louisiana 70803
(888) 882-8918
www.Lazaron.com

National Association of Professional Pet Sitters (NAPPS)
1030 15th Street NW, Suite 870
Washington, DC 20005-4709
(202) 393-3317

Pet Sitters International (PSI)
418 E. King Street
King, NC 27021-9163
(336) 983-9222 / (800) 268-7487

Pet Tech, Inc.
5965 Severin Drive, Ste. 186
La Mesa, CA 91942
(877) 865-5893

Business 9
Homemade Booklets

Go to your local bookstore and look at the "how-to" book section. You'll be surprised at how big it is. You'll find everything from "how to buy and sell used cars" to "how to raise bees for profit." People enjoy learning how to do things for themselves. That's why these books are a multi-billion dollar industry.

Now, let me tell you about a much bigger market for "how-to" books. It's a market where the books never reach the stores. A market where you can make over a million dollars - easily.

It's called the "homemade booklet market." The idea is simple. You sell information to the public through mail order. Many more people buy "how-to" information through the mail than at the store. Libraries buy it, also. Mail order fortunes are being made every month. And yet, you never hear about them.

How much can you make? Take libraries, alone. There are over 110,000 libraries that purchase books. If you sold your booklet for $39.95 to just 10 percent of those libraries, you would make $439,450.

Follow these simple steps and you will see that you have everything it takes to start your own booklet business. You don't need any special skill. It won't cost you much. In short, there's no reason why you can't become rich in this field.

CHOOSE A TOPIC

You need a topic to write about. Glance through the magazines at the supermarket check-out register. Look at the ads. The items in those ads are selling. They are the ideas people are interested in. Those popular magazines are your best resource.

Find the underlying ideas behind successful topics. They are the usual hopes and dreams of everyone. They are things like health, security, beauty, success, self-esteem and money. These are the ideas behind such hot topics as weight-loss, miracle cures, the stock market, auto detailing, organic gardening, constructing PVC furniture and how to make money on the Internet.

You could write about something you already know. The topic should be popular. It should be easy enough for your customers to do themselves.

If you're not an expert on the topic, interview people who are. People love to talk about their work. The U.S. Government has experts you may interview. Read books and magazines at the library. Get as much information as you can from the Internet, seminars and adult education classes.

WRITE THE BOOKLET

Writing the booklet is not difficult.

Decide what you are going to write about. Is it something you already know a lot about? Or will you have to research it?

Here are some topics that are popular:
- How to run a (...) business
- How to meet the love of your life
- 7 Secrets to looking younger
- How to lose weight

Learn everything you can about your topic so you can tell someone else about it. The key to success is to fill your book with good, honest information that the reader can use.

Research the competition. Are there other books on your topic? If there are, it means it's popular. That is to your advantage.

Once you have finished your research, divide your notes under different chapter headings. Write short, clear sentences. Write as if you are carrying on a conversation with a friend. The booklet does not have to be more than fifty to sixty pages long.

Read the finished booklet several times and make corrections. Let someone else read it, as well.

If you cannot write the booklet yourself, hire a ghostwriter. They are listed in writers' magazines, such as *Writer's Digest*.

MAKE THE BOOKLET

Print out the finished copy of your booklet on a laser printer. Take it to an office supply store and get a few copies reproduced. If it is fifty to sixty pages long, print it on one side only. Use a clear plastic cover for the front and the back and have it bound with a spiral plastic binder.

ADVERTISE

Place small classified ads in magazines.
Here are some good ones:
- Moneymaking Opportunities
- Spare Time
- Popular Mechanics

A lot of opportunity seekers read them.

The classified ad should be about twelve to fourteen words long. It should start with an exciting benefit, tell what you're selling and ask the reader to write you for free details. Then, reply with a sales letter. Your letter tells all the benefits the reader will get by ordering your booklet. Enclose an order form.

To get a discount in your advertising, form your own advertising agency. Give it a name and address that is separate from that of your business and buy letterhead.

Look into getting your ad on the Internet *Yellow Pages* for your area. It is a guide to local businesses.

PRICING

People sell homemade booklets for a range of prices. Most often, you'll see $19.96 to $39.95. The nice thing is that they cost so little to make. Your biggest costs are advertising and mailing out the booklets.

SIDE BUSINESSES

Now, here's the part where you can make your profits soar.

- Kits are a white-hot item. They sell like crazy. You can offer them through a catalogue or sell them separately. Gardening kits for children contain packets of seeds, gloves and plastic tools. Paper jewelry kits are popular as are kits for applying gold leaf. Furniture refinishing kits are hot.

- Audio CDs and video cassettes are great sellers. You can do anything with them. If your subject is crafts, you could show how to make the finished pieces on a video.

- Reports are in demand. They are typically two or three pages on some topic related to your booklet. You can write them fast, staple them and sell them for $7 to $10. You will make money on the high volume.

- Consulting is a big money-maker, particularly if you are an expert in your field. Big business is outsourcing these days and they need experts to come in and advise or manage whole areas of their work. You can even become a consultant for the government.

- A catalogue with several items for sale could make you big money. The items ought to have some connection to your booklet. For instance, if your topic is organic gardening, you might want to sell beneficial insects, gardening gloves, seeds and planters, etc. When you receive an order for your booklet, send out a catalogue in the same package.

- Other people's products can make you rich. If you see a book you like, contact the publisher. You ought to get a discount of 50 percent to 60 percent.

Do you see how easy it is to get in on this profitable business? The only difficult part is convincing yourself to do it. Don't wait. You have knowledge and experience to offer. People want to learn from you and they will buy your booklet.

WHAT TO DO

Find a topic
Research the topic and conduct interviews
Write the booklet or hire a ghost writer
Copyright your booklet
Hire a copywriter to write a sales letter and ads
Form an S corporation or LLC
Obtain a mailbox address
Open a business banking account
Place classified ads for inquiries
Send out sales letter to each inquiry

RESOURCES

National Association of Desktop Publishers
1260 Boylston St.
Boston, MA 02205
(617) 426-2085

National Association of Independent Publishers
   (NAIP)
P.O. Box 430
Highland City, FL 33846-0430
(863) 648-4420

Newsletter & Electronic Publishers Association
1501 Wilson Blvd., Ste. 509
Arlington, VA 22209-2403
(703) 527-2333

Poynter, Dan. *The Self-Publishing Manual.*
Santa Barbara, CA, Para Publishing, 2000.

Publishers Marketing Association
627 Aviation Way
Manhattan Beach, CA 90266
(310) 372-2732

SPAN (Small Publishers' Association of North
   America)
P.O. Box 1306
425 Cedar Street
Buena Vista, CO 81211
(719) 395-4790

Business 10
Wellness Specialist

It's nice to be wanted. And right now businesses want you if you are a wellness specialist. Almost all companies need you. Companies with a few employees all the way up to the Fortune 500.

The need for wellness specialists keeps growing. It is projected that this will be one of the top businesses throughout the 21st century.

As a wellness specialist, set up a fitness program for employees. Include exercises and nutrition information. Some wellness programs offer meditation to relieve stress. Some give counseling.

In a manufacturing company, be sure the employer informs workers of chemicals being used according to OSHA's HazCom standard rules.

Another part of your wellness program might involve ergonomics. Ergonomics means adapting the workplace to make the worker comfortable on the job. This might be simply giving employees an adjustable chair and adjustable computer screen.

A wellness program for employees is commonly

known as an Employee Assistance Program, or EAP.

EAPs go back to the early 20th century. Macy's in New York had one for their employees before 1920. EAPs lost popularity until the 1970's when the federal government funded programs to combat employee alcoholism.

Why would a business spend the extra time and money on a wellness program? That's simple. There are two overwhelming reasons:
- The business gets more work out of healthy employees. Fewer of them stay out sick. And if they are injured, they're back on the job quicker. Health care costs drop dramatically.
- There are government regulations. The Americans with Disability Act, or ADA, says that businesses must hire the disabled. Employers must adapt the workplace and work schedules to accommodate the disabled.

WHO ARE THE DISABLED?

Besides persons with visible disabilities, the disabled include persons with high blood pressure, lower back pain or diabetes. They are the obese. They are anyone who is mentally ill.

They are also people who were formerly ill or impaired. These include:

Cancer patients in remission

Anyone misdiagnosed with depression

Anyone controlling high blood pressure with medication

Drug addicts and alcoholics who have been treated and cured (Addicts and alcoholics who remain addicted are not considered disabled.)

7 STEPS TO SETTING UP A WELLNESS PROGRAM

- Make sure the management of the company is committed to it. Have a group of four people go over your program. Include two from management and two employees.
- Include workshops for exercise, stress reduction, weight loss, cardio-pulmonary resuscitation (CPR), nutrition, childbirth and addictions.
- Use ergonomics. Incorporate comfortable workstations with frequent breaks. Workers should have access to areas with natural light and quiet surroundings. Help the employer make physical changes to accommodate the disabled.
- Invite the disabled to join the wellness program with everyone else. Be careful not to single out anyone or give any person extra help. That, itself, would be considered discrimination.
- Make sure your program is employee-directed. Use a survey to learn what employees want. Every six months send around a questionnaire to find out their reactions.
- Have a return-to-work program for ill or injured employees. Keep track of their medical progress. Encourage people to report illness

and injuries immediately. You will receive a lot of reports. However, people will be taken care of quickly and the costs will be lower.

* Offer free blood pressure, cholesterol and diabetes testing as well as TB screening. Write a medical tips column in the company's newsletter.

Workers commonly suffer from musculoskeletal disorders (MSD's) such as: Carpal tunnel syndrome, Rotator cuff syndrome, De Quervain's disease, Trigger finger, Tarsal tunnel syndrome, Sciatica, Epicondylitis, Tendonitis, Raynaud's phenomenon, Carpet layer's knee, Herniated spinal disc and low back pain.

Symptoms of these disorders include: Cramping, stiffness, burning, numbness and tingling. Also, pain in the hand or wrist, the neck or back, and the arm or shoulder. Numbness and tingling in fingers is common.

Specialists group musculoskeletal disorders under the terms, "Repetitive motion injuries" and "Cumulative trauma disorders (CTSs)."

Sufferers cite the following reasons for disorders and injuries:

Working under a rushed schedule, hazardous conditions, repetitive motion, poor lighting and computer screen glare. Also, inadequate work space, broken furniture and furniture that doesn't fit them.

In one major court battle, a well-known computer manufacturer was forced to pay a woman $5.8 million for her repetitive stress injuries.

Lower back pain is the most common disability for people 45 years old and younger. Often the person is unable to go back to work.

A wellness specialist would analyze the problem, remove the risk factors, ask the worker if the changes are helping, train employees to work safely, correct deficiencies and keep records.

Once you set up a wellness program in a company, it can pretty much run itself. In the meantime, you'll be busy taking care of your own business and setting up other programs.

The price you charge the employer depends on the size of the company you serve and the size of the wellness program. Also, it will cost the company more if you have to place one of your own people in the program to run it on a regular basis.

I urge you to require a two-year contract with the company. You should be paid every month, one month in advance.

Marketing a wellness program should not be difficult. Send a professional-looking letter and brochure to all the companies in your area. That should bring the best results.

HOW TO SELL THE PROGRAM TO EMPLOYERS

Your selling points to employers are hard to resist. They include:

    Employers will get increased productivity at a lower cost.

    Fewer workers will be lost to disability.

    Companies will be complying with government regulations.

It won't be necessary to build an in-house gym.

It won't be necessary to pay health club memberships for the employees at outside health clubs.

In addition, studies indicate that employees are less likely to go to a lawyer if their company shows concern for their injury. Injured employees also return to work faster. This caring for the injured is known as "the halo effect."

SIDE BUSINESSES

- **Ergonomics consultant.** As an ergonomics consultant, your job is to help a company create a safer workplace for employees. This means reducing injury including repetitive stress injury and muscle, lower back and eye strain. You might design new workstations with proper furniture, lighting and equipment. The best products are adjustable so the worker can move the computer screen, keyboard and seating, for example. As of now, there are no special federal requirements or license to be an ergonomics consultant.

    Your best customer is the government. They have hundreds of thousands of people sitting at workstations all day. Also, most companies with employees need you. They want healthy, productive workers. In addition, the US Occupational Safety and Health Administration (OSHA) is forcing companies to comply with a torrent of new workplace regulations.

Profits are high in this business, especially if you supply special ergonomic furniture and lighting. These are high-ticket items. Also, offer an information service to inform companies of new OSHA regulations.

Think of going global with your ergonomic furniture and products.

- **Wellness consultant.** Companies would hire a wellness consultant to advise them on mental health in the workplace. This may include surveying employees and getting their input about job satisfaction, socializing and privacy concerns especially with telephone ads and e-mail.

  A consultant may offer the company advice about how to gain employee support and avoid theft, sabotage or workplace violence.

- **Newsletter publisher.** Companies would welcome a newsletter with up-dates about workplace safety and new OSHA guidelines. A newsletter could be online as well as hard copy.

WHAT TO DO

Form an S corporation or LLC
Buy insurance
Contact the groups under "Resources"
Hire an answering service
Obtain a mailbox service and use their address
Find out about government regulations
Decide on your program and your price

Make the Money and Run

Hire a booth at several trade fairs to market yourself

Send out advertising

RESOURCES

AliMed
www.alimed.com
(For ergonomic products)

Disability Rights Education and Defense Fund (DREDF)
2212 Sixth St.
Berkeley, CA 94710
(800) 466-4ADA

ErgoPro
www.ergopro.com
(For ergonomics workshops)

National Safe Workplace Institute (NSWI)
2201 Coronation Blvd., Ste. 145
Charlotte, NC 28227

National Safety Council (NSC)
1121 Spring Lake Drive
Itasca, IL 60143-3201
(630) 285-1121

North American Directory of Ergonomic Professionals and Services
www.officeorganix.com/directorye.htm
(List yourself here.)

Make the Money and Run 111

Occupational Safety & Health Administration
  (OSHA)
200 Independence Ave. SE, Rm. 715H
Washington, DC 20559
(202) 401-0721

The Wellness Council of America
Immanuel Medical Center
7105 Newport Ave.
Omaha, NE 68122
(402) 572-2900

Business 11
Private Detective

How would you like to have lunch on a sunny veranda in Katmandu? Or sail into Tangier at sunset on the trail of a kidnapped executive?

If following leads - that may take you from the dining car of the Orient Express to the tennis courts of an exclusive club in Geneva - suits you, then try the James Bond life of a "private eye."

Expect to make a lot of money. A few hundred dollars an hour plus expenses is not excessive. Your annual income can easily top several hundred thousand dollars.

Why so high? There aren't enough private detectives. Add to that the fact that crime is soaring and you have a business opportunity handed to you on a silver platter.

And, it isn't all legwork.

The computer has made a lot of the tough legwork easier. Private detectives are online. They access databases with public records that tell everything about us. Where and when you were born, where and when you married and how many children you have. Your military service, where you worked, arrests, prison, speeding tickets are all there.

Plus, there are databases that only licensed private detectives can access.

Here are some of the most profitable areas to get into:

Trade secrets is a money maker. You've seen the news. A high ranking company official steals the company's trade secrets and sells them to the competition. Every day, hundreds of trade secrets are stolen. Often the thieves are foreign governments. Companies will pay almost anything to get their secrets back.

Insurance fraud is skyrocketing. There are many fraudulent claims. It's hard for insurance companies to deal with them all. One disbarred attorney I know has his wife "fall" again and again on city property. The city always settles and provides him with a good income.

Electronic bank robbery shows that crime pays. An average heist nets the robber $250,000, according to the F.B.I. and banking security sources. Less than two percent of the robbers get caught and, of those, less than one percent go to jail.

Contrast this with robbers who hold up a bank in person. Their average take is a mere $7,500. And 80 percent of them land in jail.

Criminal hackers who commit electronic crimes are called "crackers." From an armchair anywhere in the world, they reach across the globe through their computer and steal millions of dollars. After that, they just log off. If they find that you are onto them, they destroy your computer hard drive. This leaves your system paralyzed. It's impossible to pick them up again.

Commercial truck theft is big. A truck is worth more than a car. The thief can get far more money in the stolen-parts market for a transmission from a $100,000 truck than for one from an expensive car. And it does not have to be a new truck, either.

BECOMING A PRIVATE DETECTIVE

How do you become a private detective? Check your state's licensing office. You will have to pass an exam.

To prepare for the exam, take any of the following steps:

- Look for a local private investigator to take you on as an apprentice for a couple of months. This is the best training you can receive.
- Apply for the job of apprentice investigator in an attorney's office. Choose the kind of cases you want to handle as a private detective and go to an attorney who specializes in them.
- If you cannot find a private investigator or attorney who is willing to take you on, attend classes in an accredited private detective school.

Read as much as you can about private investigation.

Some states require experience in law enforcement or private investigation. If you have been in the military or worked with the police on the regular or volunteer force, it may count. Being a security guard may also qualify you. Anyone with a criminal record may be disqualified, however.

Once licensed, you may need to be bonded. Also, buy insurance coverage including general liability.

Then, look into getting a permit to carry a gun.

Join a trade association. The other members of the association may be more help to you than anyone. They can tell you exactly what the requirements are in your state. Also, they can direct you to training courses if they are necessary. They may even be able to get you part-time employment so that you can qualify for a license in your state.

Now that you're ready to take on cases, my advice is to specialize. It will get you where you want to go much faster.

If you choose insurance fraud, for instance, apply for a job as a claims investigator with an insurance company. The insurance company may want to prove that a claim is fraudulent. This might be a case of a worker who claims he or she hurt his or her back. Your job is to catch the worker lifting heavy objects. This means long surveillance in a parked car with a video camera.

If you start your own business, work out of your home. Use a post office box for your address and hire a telephone answering service.

Advertise for clients in the *Yellow Pages*. Also, use topping. This is where your ads are carried on top of taxicabs.

A good way to get publicity is to register as a teacher in an adult education course. The pay is not high but it will make your name known in the area. It will also help you when you are applying for a license and a gun permit.

Once you have a few clients, it may be time to hire an assistant. Check out the person's background and do a credit check. If the person is not a licensed private detective, make sure he or she has law enforcement experience and can pass the exam.

SIDE BUSINESSES

Side businesses can be even more intriguing than working solely as a private detective. They also can be very lucrative.

Here are some ideas:

- **Computer security consultant.** If you have a background in computers, companies would want to hire you to set up and maintain their computer security. One way to keep a company's data secure is to use a special computer just for online communication.

- **Industrial espionage investigator.** This involves investigating the theft of trade secrets. A company, a country or a criminal gang will steal the secrets of a particular company. Companies pay a fortune to prevent such theft.

- **Consultant to companies.** As a consultant, you would have an area of expertise. For instance, you might train management how to avoid violence in the workplace. This is a growing problem that is being swept under the rug. Yet, all companies worry about it. The cases usually involve injury, destruction of property and even death.

- **Background investigator.** Specializing in background investigations and credit checks is very profitable. Companies will turn to you before they hire an employee.

WHAT TO DO

Talk with private detectives about the work

Check with your state's licensing office

Join a trade association

Work with a private investigator

Take an exam if required

Gain experience by working with investigator/attorney

Decide on a specialty

Apply for a license if required

Form an S corporation or LLC

Buy insurance

Apply for a gun permit

Advertise

RESOURCES

International Security and Detective Alliance (ISDA)
P.O. Box 6303
Corpus Christi, TX 78466-6303
(512) 888-6164

ION
P.O. Box 40970
Mesa, AZ 85274-0970
(800) 338-3463

National Association of Investigative Specialists
P.O. Box 33244
Austin, TX 78764
(512) 719-3595

World Association of Detectives
P.O. Box 441000-301
Aurora, CO 80044
(800) 962-0516

World Investigators Network
P.O. Box 0656
Baltimore, MD 21219
(410) 477-8879

Business 12
Place a Chef

I found out something astounding a while ago. And I've been carrying it around like a deep secret. I've had no one to tell it to. Until now. . . .

Here it is:

Putting a chef to work can make you rich.

"Hmmm," you might say, "what kind of secret is that? Besides, what do I know about chefs?"

That's just the point. You don't need to know anything about them—except the salaries they make in your area. Where I live, a good chef in a French restaurant earns about $250,000 a year.

Let me tell you how I found out that getting a chef a job is a gold-mine. I worked for an executive search firm. We found jobs for managers and other high-level administrative people. That was our main work. But we had a sideline—*chefs*. And, they were our big money-maker.

We looked all over the world for chefs. If a restaurant needed a top French chef, we contracted with a search firm in France to find one. At first, the restaurants who hired us were in our area. But soon, restaurants elsewhere wanted us to find them a chef.

Our commission was negotiable. It depended on how well-known the chef was and how badly the restaurant needed him or her. On some placements we received 30 percent to 40 percent of the first year's salary. On others, it was just one or two months' salary.

We were paid by the restaurant. The chef paid nothing. We earned $25,000 to $125,000 for a chef. And, we were paid up front. The chef had to sign a year's contract with the restaurant. But if he or she left in less than a year, we still were paid.

You can do the same thing.

START YOUR OWN BUSINESS

Image is everything in this business. Hire a professional to design letterhead, a brochure and business cards.

Set up an S corporation or LLC. Give your company a French name.

Use a mail box service and put the street address as your business address.

FINDING CLIENTS

Start with the end-user first—the restaurants. Research all the high-priced restaurants in your area. Meet with their managers. Explain your service and ask them if they would be interested in having you find a chef for them.

One great advantage you have is that chefs change jobs a lot. So restaurants are always in the market for a new one.

Join the National Restaurant Association and advertise in trade journals. Join the local merchants groups and the Better Business Bureau.

EXPAND OVER THE COUNTRY

Set up a Web site. It's vital that you have your message on the Internet.

Use direct mail. Have a sales letter professionally written on quality letterhead. Enclose your brochure and business card. You should have a toll-free number. It's important, also, to hire a 24-hour answering service to take all your calls.

Have a mailing service send the letter out to 6000 of the highest priced restaurants in the country. Concentrate on New York City, San Francisco, Chicago and Miami.

Go to trade shows. You will find restaurants that will use your service. And you'll find chefs. Rent a booth at the show and hand out information about your service. Give away premiums such as pot holders, chefs' toques or kitchen utensils with your logo. Meet and talk with restaurant owners.

FINDING CHEFS

To reach chefs, contact cooking schools. Ask for a list of their students who have graduated or are about to graduate. Contact schools in the United States and in Europe.

Join several trade associations. Besides the National Restaurant Association, join an umbrella organization such as the National Business Association, the Direct Marketing Association and the Chamber of Commerce. Trade organizations can help with licensing, insurance and marketing.

SIDE BUSINESSES

Among the side businesses, two stand out as being particularly profitable. You might choose one as your full-time business.

> ➤ **Rent a chef.** This is a flourishing business in many cities. It works like this:

You would advertise gourmet meals prepared and delivered by a personal chef. Who wouldn't love to come home to a home-made gourmet meal.

As a personal chef, you would plan menus with the customer. Then, you would shop, cook and freeze the meals. The meals should be packaged in microwave oven safe containers. Include a label on each meal, listing the contents. Place the meals in a freezer immediately on arriving at a customer's home. Plan to deliver enough meals for ten to fifteen days in advance.

Find out how to price meals in your area by checking with the U.S. Personal Chef Association. Your minimum service should be one month, payable in advance. Advertise your service on the Internet. Do local radio spots. Send news releases to the local newspaper.

Check with your trade association about local laws. Some areas require that food for sale be prepared in a commercial kitchen. This could even be in a diner. Hire an assistant chef to help you or your main chef. Line up delivery people with transportation.

> **Food delivery from area restaurants.** This is a popular trend all over the country. Many people do not eat in a restaurant. They prefer to eat restaurant food at home. About one in ten restaurant meals is served by a delivery service.

Here are some steps to take:

First, line up as many clients as possible. Then, visit restaurants that are already participating in take-out delivery. Inquire if they would work with you on the same terms as other take-out delivery services.

Work out a menu with the restaurants. Then, print it up on flyers that you deliver to homes and offices.

Line up delivery people with their own transportation.

Your office would be in contact with the delivery people by cell phone and pagers.

Your customers pay the regular restaurant prices. But you pay the restaurant a discount price. The difference is your profit. Customers would also pay a service charge of $3.95 on all orders from any one restaurant plus a driver's tip.

This business has skyrocketing profit potential. If you make 1000 deliveries a day and net $8 a delivery, that's $8,000 a day. Multiply this by seven days a week and you have around $56,000 a week. That works out to nearly $3 million a year!

Today, nobody has time to cook. What an opportunity for you.

WHAT TO DO

Survey the number of restaurants in your area
Is there a high turnover in chefs
Could you do better going national
Set up an S corporation or LLC
Have an attorney draw up a contract for your use
Go to restaurant trade shows
Contact restaurants
Contact cooking schools
Launch a direct mail campaign

RESOURCES

American Culinary Federation (ACF)
10 San Bartola Rd.
Post Office Box 3466
St. Augustine, FL 32085
(904) 824-4468

American Personal Chef Institute
4572 Delaware Street
San Diego, CA 92116
(800) 644-8389

Chefs de Cuisine Association of America
155 E. 55th St., Ste. 302B
New York, NY 10022
(212) 832-4939

Food Marketing Institute
800 Connecticut Ave. NW, Ste. 500
Washington, DC 20006
(202) 452-8444

National Restaurant Association
1200 17th St. NW
Washington, DC 20036-3097
(202) 331-5900

U.S. Personal Chef Association
481 Rio Rancho Blvd., NE
Rio Rancho, NM 87114
(800) 995-2138

Business 13
Diaries

What if I told you I have the perfect business for you? Imagine a business that is easy to run, has a simple product and can make you staggering amounts of money. And, of course, it's legal.

Well, I've found it!

It's *diaries*.

See what you think.

First of all, I cannot take credit for this idea. It all goes to my old friend, Alex, who ran a gift album business. Read through the chapter "Gift Albums" to find out how you can get rich in that business, also.

After Alex had made his fortune in gift albums, he wanted to try something else. He wanted to see if his system that had worked so well with albums would work with another product.

His system followed two easy steps. Here it is:

- Find a product
- Get someone else to pay for it

The new product wasn't hard to find. It was a diary.

Alex had a plan. He would make a simple golf diary. He knew a little about golf and he saw that a lot of other people were interested in it.

The main thing was, he didn't want to risk his fortune in case the product didn't sell. So he decided to get someone else to help foot the costs right from the start.

Alex didn't expect to make as much money with the diary as he did with the album. He just wanted to test his system and this seemed like a low-risk venture. He didn't expect to become a millionaire all over again. But that is exactly what happened.

And you can do the same thing.

Here's how he did it.

THE DIARY

Alex researched the product. He didn't have to look far. All the people he knew consulted diaries. They called them planners, agenda, calendars, diaries or appointment books. But they all served the same purpose. They planned a person's day.

He looked up diary manufacturers in the Thomas Register at the library and contacted them.

The size of the diary was important. The pages would be 5½" by 8½", or "journal-size." The cover would be 6½" by 9½". He didn't want it too small as he intended to include pages of golf photos. Also, it had to be just the right size to carry in a briefcase and fit easily in a narrow drawer.

The cover, he knew, would have to be leather-like vinyl. Leather, itself, was too expensive and too heavy. He needed something light-weight that he could send through the mail at a reasonable cost. For that is how he intended to sell the diary—through mail order.

The color of the cover was important. The three most asked-for colors for appointment books are dark tan, burgundy and black—in that order. Initials could be stamped in gold on the lower right hand corner if customers were willing to pay a few extra dollars.

The pages would be spiral bound to allow the diary to lie flat when open. The spiral binding would be inside the cover and not visible when the diary was closed.

The diary would be a weekly planner. When it lay open, the right-hand page would have the seven days of the week printed down the right margin. To the left of each day there would be plenty of space for the owner to write in. Thin lines across the page would separate the days.

On the left-hand page, Alex decided to place photographs. And here is where it became interesting. He contacted golf equipment companies and told them of his diary. He also wrote to sports clubs, golf course management companies and famous golfers, themselves.

Soon, he got all the pictures he wanted. Some of them were autographed by golf stars.

The first part of Alex's system was in place. He had a simple product with appeal.

The second part of his system, someone else to pay the costs, came within weeks.

SOMEONE TO PAY THE COSTS

Golf equipment manufacturers, themselves, decided to give Alex financial backing. The pictures Alex was using showed golfers using the manufacturers' equipment. They knew this was excellent publicity.

Some of the left-hand pages had no photos. Instead, they showed golf tips and simple illustrations of how to stand and how to carry out power swings. Interesting stories about the world's greatest golfers were included, also. There was news golfers could use about upcoming tournaments, golf courses and new technology in golf clubs.

At the back of the diary was an address book and an expense and reimbursement record. There were also blank pages for notes.

MARKETING THE DIARY

Alex initially ordered 5000 diaries. This fast turned out to be a drop in the bucket. They sold out. He reordered another 10,000 and then 50,000 and more after that.

His main method of sales was through mail order. He placed classified ads in golf magazines. He did a two-step ad. Respondents would write to his post office box or telephone his toll-free number. He would send them a sales letter. He offered a pen as a free gift if they ordered before a certain date.

He also sold his diary through golf clubs. He gave them 50 percent of the sales price on all diaries sold. In addition, he sold quite a few through golf equipment stores and department stores.

One of his biggest sales outlets was two catalogue houses. They sold many thousands of his diaries. He offered them a generous discount of 70 percent. That fired them up to renew their contract with him year after year.

No one was more bowled over by the success of the diary than Alex, himself. But, as he says, no matter how many diaries there are out there, there is always room for more. People love diaries. They want to feel organized.

Diary companies like Alex's are making billions of dollars a year. One company, I know well, has over 4 million customers. With prices ranging from around $16 to $140, you can see what I mean about making a fortune.

You can do the same thing Alex did. He chose a niche market which was golfers. It turned out to be a winner and he stayed with it for years. Golfers, he found, bought anything connected with their sport. Other popular subjects are:

- Cars—sports models and antique cars
- Stock Market
- Baseball
- Kittens
- Weight-Loss

A weight loss diary could be a tremendous money-maker. You could include low calorie, healthy recipes for each day. Add a daily motivational thought to keep the dieter's spirits up.

Once your diary business has taken off and you are making money, add related items to your catalogue. Here are a few fast-selling products:

- Pens

Wallets, credit card holders

Slim calculators

Organizers with a diary, calculator, credit card holder, vinyl pockets for stamps and clips, small stapler and photo holder

Small digital clocks

Whatever you choose, I know you'll be a success. I'll be looking for your diaries soon.

WHAT TO DO

Find a good subject for your diary

Contact companies in the Thomas Register

Look at diaries in stores and catalogues

Write to manufacturers for photos

Design your diary or have a professional do it

Hire a copywriter write a sales letter and ads

Form an S corporation or LLC

Have a small run of diaries manufactured

Place ads in specialty magazines

Ask catalogue houses and stores to carry your diary

Order pens to serve as a free customer bonus

RESOURCES

American Home Business Association
4505 S. Wasatch Blvd., No. 140
Salt Lake City, UT 84124
(800) 664-2422

Lant, Jeffrey. *The Unabashed Self-Promoter's Guide.* Cambridge, MA, Jeffrey Lant Associates, 1983.

National Small Business Association
1155 15th St. NW
Washington, DC 20005

Sewell, Susan. *Advertising Made Easy.*
Los Angeles, Price Stern Sloan, 1990.

Thomas Register of American Manufacturers
Thomas Publishing Company
5 Penn Plaza
New York, NY 10001

Business 14
Trade Shows

Have you ever wondered who runs those big trade shows at the convention centers or in big name hotels? I never thought about it until one day when a friend of mine brought it up. He's a regular exhibitor at a minerals show.

"You know who makes all the money here, don't you?" he said. "It isn't any of us," he went on, cocking his chin at the other exhibitors. "It's David K., the manager of this whole business. He's got more gold than Midas. And, do you know where he is?—On the beach in Maui!"

That got me to thinking. Did David really make a lot of money putting on the trade show? I mulled it over a couple of months until I had a chance to do some research. What I discovered astounded me. David was making over $1.5 million dollars a year on his shows. And, he wasn't alone. Other trade show management companies were making 15 times that.

I couldn't wait to find out how to become a trade show manager.

Make the Money and Run

Trade show managers don't like to talk about how much money they make. They would prefer to talk about the work they do. The shows they put on are like a circus and they are the ring master. They told me it was relatively easy to break into the business.

First, I learned that the trade show industry generates $150 to $200 billion a year.

Secondly, anyone can run a trade show. It costs very little to start up. A woman in Baltimore ran a couple of craft shows a year. She started on less than $500. And, she had no experience.

She earned over $1 million in two years.

The trade show business is loaded with benefits. It has one of the largest cash flows of any business. The money comes in before you hold the show. This means you have no accounts receivable. You also have no inventory. And you don't need an office. In fact, it's better if you work out of your home.

You need to know how to organize people and events. You have to plan the show in advance. Advance planning should take 18 to 24 months.

Trade shows are popular. Companies jump at the chance to exhibit because they can find buyers at the show for their products. Some walk out with million dollar contracts and new customers that stay with them for years. Most people go to shows to find new products and check out the competition.

There are over 3700 big shows a year and at least that many small, regional shows. That's about 8000 a year and the number is growing fast.

The usual trade show lasts two to three days. It's easy to find exhibitors and once you have them, it's even easier to get people to attend.

YOUR OWN TRADE SHOW

Here's how to get into the trade show management business:

- First, do some research. Contact the Trade Show Bureau for information. They are an exposition industry research firm. They offer video and audio tapes and publications. And, they have trade show directory listings.

  Hold a business to business trade show. They are less work than the consumer shows. Also, you make more money since you can charge exhibitors more. You have a smaller, more focused group of buyers. And there are fewer security problems.

- The next step is to decide which industry you want to focus on. Choose those industries where there are already a lot of trade shows. It indicates interest. Here are some industry shows in order of popularity:
  - Medical and health care
  - Computer and software
  - Home furnishings and interior design
  - Sporting goods and recreation
  - Education
  - Building and construction
  - Agriculture and farming
  - Apparel

- Target a small niche. For instance, if you choose home furnishings, you could hold a show on how to produce a catalogue. Your exhibitors would be printers, designers, copywriters, mailing service and order service companies and dropshippers.

- Contact industry trade associations and ask them for support. Assure them you are not competing with their show. You'll hold your show at a different time and place from theirs.
- Plan at least eighteen months in advance. You need that much time to rent exhibition space in a hotel. In addition, it takes a few months to test the idea of your trade show.
- Locate about 200 companies to exhibit. Send them a professional-looking brochure and letter. A mailing list company can provide you with a tightly-focused list of people most likely to exhibit.

  Market to people who are likely to attend. Send them free tickets.
- Once you have 80 to 100 exhibitors and a good response from prospective attendees, line up a time and place for your show.

The best place is in a hotel on the outskirts of a big city. Renting a convention center inside the city is phenomenally expensive and difficult to book. The big trade shows have convention centers booked years in advance.

Chances are, the hotel won't charge you for the exhibition room if exhibitors or attendees stay in rooms at the hotel.

The top ten convention cities in order of importance are:

Chicago
Atlanta
Toronto
New York City

Orlando
Las Vegas
Dallas
San Francisco
Washington, DC
Boston

The best time for a show is when other conventions are not being held. Also, avoid holding a show during the snowy season or a holiday week.

- Ask for written commitments from exhibitors and ask them for their table fees immediately. These can be several thousand dollars per exhibitor. The fee includes table, electricity, clean-up, advertising and a list of show attendees. Ask exhibitors to send free tickets to their own customers.

- Plan events such as seminars, films, speakers, demonstrations and dinners.

- Market the show to your target audience. Narrow your advertising focus so you don't squander your money. Place ads in the right magazines and trade journals.

  Business trade shows do not charge an entrance fee. There usually is an admission fee to consumer shows.

- As an added incentive to attend, include a drawing and several door prizes. Offer refreshments.

- Hire a firm to register people at the door and give out badges. This firm would produce a computerized list of attendees for you.

A big secret to success: Start small and set up a trade show that you are interested in. Because, if it is a success, you will be expected to put it on year after year.

SIDE BUSINESSES

Side business opportunities spring up by themselves.

- **List Rental.** Rent your lists of exhibitors and attendees. The lists are current, active and valuable. Tens of thousands of companies around the world will want to rent them from you.
- **Videotapes.** Videotape the trade show and sell it. Hire graduate students in film-making to do the shooting. Have them sign a contract that they accept full payment in cash and will not claim royalties.
- **Premiums.** A third business is selling products such as premiums, books, CDs and videos. Offer any products you think will sell. Food, for instance, always sells.
- **Marketing consultant.** Become a marketing consultant. Set up your own booth at the trade show. Spell out the benefits you offer. Tell clients how you can boost their sales.

WHAT TO DO

Form an S corporation or LLC
Determine which industry you want to be in
Contact prospective exhibitors and attendees
Line up a hotel and a date
Contact trade organizations
Collect exhibitors' fees
Hire a firm to register attendees

RESOURCES

Exhibits Directory
Association of American Publishers
71 Fifth Ave.
New York, NY 10003
(212) 255-0200

Trade Show Bureau
1660 Lincoln St., Ste. 2080
Denver, CO 80264
(303) 860-7626

Trade Show Exhibitors Association
5501 Backlick Road, Suite 105
Springfield, VA 22151
(703) 941-3725

Tradeshow Week
R.R. Bowker
121 Chanlon Rd.
New Providence, NJ 07974
(800) 521-8110

Tradeshow Weekly Data Book
R.R. Bowker
P.O. Box 31
New Providence, NJ 07974
(888) 269-5372

Trade Shows Worldwide
The Gale Group
27500 Drake Rd.
Farmington Hills, MI 48331
(800) 877 GALE

Business 15
Regulations Specialist

Companies are being sued left and right. They are being brought to court every day by employees or customers. Or else, by the government.

The company usually agrees to pay an out of court settlement. It is cheaper than fighting the lawsuit. But often, the settlement is so large, the company is forced out of business, anyway.

This is a golden opportunity for you. You can stop the lawsuit before it begins.

As a regulations specialist, you would keep companies informed about regulations that apply to them. By following the regulations, they may be able to avoid the most common lawsuits.

Common lawsuits involve discrimination, sexual harassment, civil rights infringements, family and medical leave, safety and health standards, privacy rights and labor standards.

One of the problems for business is that the federal government constantly issues new regulations or changes the old ones. There are over 300,000 federal regulations that are criminally enforceable.

It is nearly impossible to keep up with all of them. Most small companies cannot afford to hire a full-time person to keep track of them.

You need no specific training to become a regulations specialist. You don't need a license, either. The costs for you to set up business are small.

You do not need an office. You can work from home. However, you should have a computer, a laser printer and a fax machine. It is important to be online.

There are two top-notch products you could offer. One is a poster. The other, an up-dates service.

POSTER

Hire a designer and a printer to produce a quality poster.

Send the poster to your clients. It will display the necessary notices that the federal government requires that businesses post on their bulletin board.

The poster would display the major federal acts. They include:

   Anti-Discrimination Notice
   Consolidated EEO Notice
   Employee Polygraph Protection Act
   Fair Labor Standards Act
   Family and Medical Leave Act
   Federal Minimum Wage Law
   Occupational Safety and Health
     Administration

Make the Money and Run 147

Have the poster show the current federal minimum wage.

The poster should be about 20" by 26". Big enough to fit on an average bulletin board. To keep costs down use only two colors. Use heavy-weight paper. Have it covered with a protective film. This will keep it from yellowing and allow it to be wiped clean.

UP-DATES SERVICE

Most businesses would gladly pay for an up-dates service that alerted them to changes in the law. Your job would be to keep up with issues on Capitol Hill. You might interview lawmakers and find out how these issues would affect your clients' businesses.

Regulations is one business where you can meet powerful people and get paid well for it.

An example of an up-date is the Federal Minimum Wage Law. Every business must post a notice of this law and the current wage. This is true even if a company has only one employee and he or she is making more than the minimum. Failure to post it will cost the company a heavy fine.

With your up-dates service, you may have to customize. Some regulations affect only certain industries. Thus, if your client is a printer, send him or her only those regulations that pertain to the printing industry.

Also, some regulations affect only those firms having over a certain number of employees.

Along with up-dates, fax clients new interpretations of existing laws. The Americans with Disabilities Act (ADA) of 1990 has many interpretations. Federal regulators now say that people with psychiatric disorders have the same rights as the physically handicapped. Employers must ensure that the mentally ill are not stressed.

WHERE TO GET YOUR INFORMATION

The federal government is online. You can access most of the information you need from their Web sites.

The main source for government rules is the Code of Federal Regulations. It lists regulations in the Federal Register.

Government standards and regulations change all the time even though the federal act that establishes them remains the same.

MARKETING

You provide a valuable service. Businesses will pay a high price for it. It can prevent steep fines or lawsuits. Also, it's cheaper for a business to pay for your service than to hire a law firm.

Sell your service as a membership. Customers would pay you a yearly membership fee. In return, you would send them three posters with the federal regulations. Plus, you would fax them new federal laws as they are passed. The laws that you fax to a particular client would directly affect him or her.

Offer your poster and up-dates service to firms all over the country. Advertise online. Also, use direct mail. Hire a professional copywriter to put together a sales letter and brochure. Have a mailing service send them to 5000 mid-size businesses.

When you feel secure in handling federal regulations you may want to branch out.

SIDE BUSINESSES

- **State and local regulations.** A natural extension of your business is covering state and local regulations. State and local governments work fast. They can enact a law today and have it on the books tomorrow. They produce a steady stream of regulations that is impossible for an employer to keep up with.

Yet, companies must adhere to state and local regulations as well as to federal. This means a lot of profits for you.

Here are some recent state laws that are sweeping the nation:

Anti-bias protection. This states that employers and insurers cannot employ genetic testing or the family history of candidates.

In some states, an employee seeking another job cannot sue his former boss for a reference he considers unfair.

Child labor laws are being tightened or relaxed depending on the state.

Electronic monitoring of employees by employers. Many states allow it. Currently, in Connecticut, the employer must alert the employee in writing before he or she monitors.

The minimum wage is also a hot issue. Approximately ten states as well as the District of Columbia have ruled that employers must pay more than the federal minimum wage.

Most states have sites on the Internet. They include the complete text of all their legislation. It might take you hours to read through a single text. This is too long. But, there is a short-cut.

There are three sites that cut to the quick and give you only the important facts. One is a data retrieval service called Lexis-Nexis. The second is LegiSlate, owned by the Washington Post Company. And the third is StateScape, owned by State Analysis, Inc.

Offer this service to your federal regulations clients. They may be happy to have you assist them with all regulations.

- **Videotapes.** Hire a professional studio to produce your video. Hire actors to show how to employ the handicapped or set up anti-discrimination policies. You could show your poster being put up on a bulletin board.

- **Compliance consulting.** The job of compliance consultant is to advise health care businesses and insurers about complying with Medicare regulations. This work is extremely well-paid.

  It requires an in-depth understanding of the Medicare rules. These are a tangle of federal statutes that few people fully understand. A compliance consultant would be expected to know how much the federal government is expected to reimburse the health care provider and which services should be covered.

- **Anti-discrimination consulting.** Religion in the workplace is the basis for an increasing number of lawsuits. Employees are suing their companies for the right to dress and behave according to their religious belief. The EEOC, or, Equal Employment Opportunity Commission, is ruling in these cases.

An anti-discrimination consultant would advise the employer about the latest judgements. A consultant would be expected to thoroughly understand Title VII of the 1964 Civil Rights Code. Generally, Title VII says that any ethical or moral belief a person holds can be regarded as a religion—so long as that person holds it as strongly as one would a traditionally accepted religion.

Therefore, a person may establish his or her own religion. He or she may take time off to practice it and he or she may wear religious clothing at work. OSHA, Occupational Safety and Health Administration, does not allow clothing that would pose a danger on the job.

You shouldn't have any trouble striking it rich in regulations if you take time to learn the subject. There's a long line of potential customers just waiting for you to get started.

WHAT TO DO

Form an S corporation or LLC
Hire a telephone answering service
Have a poster designed and printed
Send out direct mail ads

Subscribe to an online service
Obtain merchant status to accept credit cards
Hire a lawyer to review all documents

RESOURCES

Americans with Disabilities Act Handbook
Government Printing Office
Superintendent of Documents
Washington, DC 20402
(202) 512-1800
www.access.gpo.gov/sudocs

Code of Federal Regulations
Government Printing Office
(See above.)

Consulting Opportunities Journal
P.O. Box 430
Clear Springs, MD 21722
(301) 791-9332

Equal Employment Opportunity Commission
(EEOC)
1801 L Street, NW
Washington, DC 20507

Federal Register
Government Printing Office
(See above.)

U.S. Chamber of Commerce
1615 H Street, N.W.
Washington, DC 20062-2000

Business 16
Nonprofit

Here is a way to have your cake and eat it, too.

With a nonprofit corporation, you help someone in need and get rich doing it. Set up a good, honest charity and get paid the high salary you deserve.

There is no law stating how much money must go to the charity and how much to your salary.

Americans are a generous people. They dig into their pockets even when there's little to give. They give about $200 billion a year to charity. Around 70 percent of Americans have some connection to a nonprofit organization. Some seven million are volunteers. Another seven million work for a nonprofit.

Probably you already give to a church or donate money or clothes to a charity. Perhaps you work for a volunteer police force or fire brigade.

You can do the same good work—only, this time, you share in the good fortune.

How can you get rich with a nonprofit?

Use the benefits that the federal government allows you. Nonprofits do jobs the government doesn't want to do. Jobs such as helping the poor and taking in abandoned animals.

The government gives generous benefits. The biggest benefit is that you do not pay taxes. You are subsidized by the government. You have to apply for tax exemption.

Another benefit is low postal rates.

Also, the nonprofit decides how much income to give to the charitable cause. There is no law about this. Respected nonprofits give 60 percent to 65 percent of the money they bring in to the cause.

What exactly is a nonprofit corporation?

It is a public charity. The nonprofit corporation is a creation of the IRS and goes by the title 501(c)(3).

The 501(c)(3) is the only nonprofit organization to be truly tax exempt. The IRS says that every 501(c)(3) must have a cause that is scientific, charitable, educational or religious. Or, it must work for the prevention of cruelty to children or to animals.

There are two types of 501(c)(3):

A **private foundation**. It receives funding from one private source, usually a family.

A **public charity**. It's better to be a public charity because the IRS has much looser rules for a public charity than it does for a private foundation.

So, the easiest and best choice is to set up a 501(c)(3) public charity.

Here is how to do it:

HOW TO SET UP YOUR CHARITY

- Make sure your charitable cause fits the IRS's definition for the 501(c)(3). (See above).
- Follow these guidelines for a 501(c)(3):
  1. Must be incorporated
  2. Must have a public purpose
  3. Must preclude self interest and private financial gain
  4. Must be tax exempt
  5. Must have specific legal status so gifts are tax deductible
- Find a minimum of three like-minded people to serve on your board of directors. They must be majority age. Choose carefully, as they have the vote and can vote you out.
- Consult a lawyer specializing in nonprofits. Have him or her set up a nonprofit corporation. You can be founder and president of the board. You cannot be owner since a nonprofit has no owner.
- File the Articles of Incorporation with the state. Name a registered agent in the state to be the contact person for your nonprofit.
- Draw up bylaws. These are not filed with the state. They are internal rules telling how you operate.
- Write up the Organizational Meeting Minutes.
- Apply for Federal Tax Exemption (Form 1023) and State Tax Exemption.

- File the state's charitable solicitation registration and reports.

This may seem like a lot. But a good lawyer can have your organization up and running in a short time. The longest wait is for the IRS to grant you tax exempt status. In the meantime, you can have another 501(c)(3) receive grants in your name and pass them through to you.

HELPFUL TIPS

Here are certain interesting points about a 501(c)(3):

> The IRS says you are allowed to do only insubstantial lobbying. But they don't say exactly what "insubstantial" means. As a result, many 501(c)(3)'s have been closed down because they lobbied—even a little.

But, there is a loophole that can keep you out of trouble. Ask your lawyer to elect the 501(H) option. File Form 5768 and elect to use the limits on lobbying expenditures. With this option, you can spend 15 percent to 20 percent of your money on lobbying. If you exceed that amount three to four years in a row, you pay a fine.

You may think that you will never do any lobbying. But, you'll probably find yourself slipping into lobbying. For instance, it's natural to lobby for animal welfare if your organization helps animals.

One thing a 501(c)(3) should never do is campaign for or against a political candidate. It will lose its status.

Make the Money and Run 157

- A nonprofit should make a profit. The restriction is on how you use that profit. Use it for your organization's cause. If money is left over at the end of the year, plow it back into the organization.
- Bonuses are tricky. You cannot use your net income at year end to give out bonuses to your employees or yourself.
- Always make your 501(C)(3) "perpetual." That gives you the right to dissolve it when you choose to. If you do dissolve it, the money left over must go to another 501(c)(3).
- Do not put your own assets into your nonprofit. You cannot take them back out.
- A 501(c)(3) has to be a C corporation. An S corporation or a limited liability company cannot be a 501(c)(3).
- You have little control over your nonprofit once it is set up. The board of directors governs it. The board of directors has the vote. It can vote you out. It also has the right to reelect itself.

One way to control your board is to appoint yourself, relatives and friends to it. You can be both a board member and an employee of the nonprofit.

However, you cannot vote your own salary. Anyone on the board who is related to you cannot set your salary, either. The board has to base your salary on what other directors are earning.

The president of the board determines the salaries of the officers.

- If you have membership, do not give members

the vote. Otherwise, they can vote you out of office.

➤ Set up an advisory board of prominent people. It is purely an honorary position. They do not govern nor do they vote. List their names on your letterhead and all publicity. Prominent people make your organization look important.

RAISING MONEY

- Fund raising is a major activity of any nonprofit. Money comes from federal, state and local government and from foundations and corporations.
- Another successful means of obtaining money is through direct mail to wealthy individuals. Rent lists of people who have donated money to other charities, similar to yours.
- A third way of getting funding is cause marketing. Endorse a product of a major company and let them pay you for it.
- Hire a well-respected fund raising company to raise money for you. To find one, check with the Support Center of America.
- Side businesses will bring in money. Set up a for-profit corporation and donate the profits to your nonprofit. Any side business is fine. It doesn't have to be in the same area as your nonprofit.
- Become a fund raiser, yourself. Take a course in fund raising from the Support Center of America

or the Foundation Center. You can make money raising funds for other nonprofits.

WHAT TO DO

Set up a 501(c)(3) corporation with an attorney
File for federal tax exempt status (Form 1023)
Register in your state
File for state income tax exemption
Apply for special bulk, 3rd class postal rates
File state charitable solicitation registration and reports
Obtain state immunity protecting volunteers from liability
Buy general liability insurance
Buy directors and officers insurance

RESOURCES

American Institute of Philanthropy
4579 Laclede Ave.
St. Louis, MO 63108

American Prospect Research Association
414 Plaza Drive, Ste 209
Westmont, IL 60559

American Society of Association Executives (ASAE)
1575 I St. NW
Washington, DC 20005-1168
(202) 626-2723

Make the Money and Run

Annual Register of Grant Support 2001
R.R. Bowker
P.O. Box 31
New Providence, NJ 07974
(888) 269-5372

The Foundation Center
79 Fifth Ave.
New York, NY 10003-3076

National Council of Nonprofit Associations
1001 Connecticut Ave., NW, Ste. 900
Washington, DC 20036

National Federation of Nonprofits
815 15th St., NW, Ste. 822
Washington, DC 20001-2201
(202) 628-4380

Society for Nonprofit Organizations (SNPO)
6314 Odana Rd., Ste. 1
Madison, WI 53719
(608) 274-9777

The Support Center of America
National Office: (415) 552-7660

Business 17
Information Broker

How curious are you?... Very?...Somewhat?... Do you work well alone or do you have to have someone supervising you? Can you work odd hours or are you set into a nine to five schedule?

If you answered "yes" to the first half of each question, you have what it takes to be an information broker.

An information broker buys and sells information. Years ago, you either had to hire researchers to find information or track it down, yourself.

Today that same information comes through an online service. All information brokers today are online.

The value of an information broker is that he or she puts the information in a form that the client can use.

A famous information broker is Andrew Garvin. He was at Columbia University's School of Journalism in the 1960's when he founded FIND/SVP. He began in his apartment with $12,000. Today, FIND/

SVP is a multi-million dollar information company.
You can do the same thing. There is a tremendous demand for information.

STARTING YOUR BUSINESS

First, choose your buyers. Who are you going to sell to? Focus on one narrow group.

Finding a niche for yourself is 90 percent of your success.

Next, start small, the way Andrew Garvin did.

Work from home. Hire a secretarial service to answer the phone and receive mail. You'll need a computer, a printer and a fast modem.

How much will you charge? Find out what other information services are charging in your area and copy them.

Do not take a customer on credit in this profession. You won't be paid. And it's impossible to take back information.

FINDING CUSTOMERS

It's time to contact clients. Here are a few ideas:
- Set up your own Web site.
- Offer a free consultation to prospective clients.
- Use direct mail. Rent a list of people who work in your niche field. Hire a copywriter to make a professional looking mail piece. Send it out to everyone on the list.
- Join a trade association, the Better Business

Bureau and the Chamber of Commerce. Membership makes you look solid.
- Be sure to get a business telephone listing so that you are in the white pages and the *Yellow Pages*.
- Line up references. Good ones are your attorney, accountant and other business people. When you get your first client, ask him or her for an endorsement.

HELPFUL HINTS

Soon, you'll have clients calling you regularly. Work will increase as word gets around about your service. Old clients will refer new ones to you.

As you accept jobs, keep asking yourself these two key questions:

What is my client paying me for?

How does my client intend to use this information?

They are vital questions. The answers should be spelled out in the contract between you and your client. You should know exactly what is expected of you.

Many information specialists work night and day on a big project. They gather information and repackage it for the client. The next thing they know, the client tells them he can't use it. It isn't what he asked for. They have missed the point entirely. Often, the whole job has to be scrapped.

The core of the information broker's job is repackaging information.

This means putting raw data into a form that your

client can use.

Gather facts from different sources and find a connection that no one else has seen. This is why you want to know how the client intends to use the information.

When business builds up, hire graduate students to help you. Make sure they are independent contractors.

SIDE BUSINESSES

Here are some ways to branch out and double your profits:

- ➤ Research reports. They sell for thousands of dollars. Send out a catalogue of your reports and those of others.
- ➤ Consulting. If you specialize in a field, charge a high hourly rate as a consultant.
- ➤ Pay-per-call service. If you specialize in information that changes regularly, set up a hot line with updates. The telephone company will bill the callers for you.

One of the hottest items for the pay-per-call business is astrology charts. There is software that will chart the information for you.

There's room for everybody in the information business. You just have to find your special area. And, like Andrew Garvin, you may end up at the head of a multi-million dollar business. Why not?

When I need information, I'll come to you.

WHAT TO DO

Specialize in one area
Purchase computer equipment
Go online and set up a Web site
Become familiar with databases
Set up an S corporation or LLC
Join two trade associations
Hire a secretarial service
Send out mailings to prospective clients

RESOURCES

Association of Independent Information
 Professionals
10290 Monroe No. 208
Dallas, TX 75229
(469) 730-8759

Association for Information & Image Management
1100 Wayne Ave., Ste. 1100
Silver Spring, MD 20910
(301) 587-8202

Association of Records Managers and
 Administrators (ARMA International)
4200 Somerset, Ste. 215
Prairie Village, KS 66208
(913) 341-3808 / (800) 422-2762

DIALOG Information Services
3460 Hillview Ave.
Palo Alto, CA 94324
(800) 334-2564

LEXIS/NEXIS
Mead Data Central
P.O. Box 933
Dayton, OH 45401
(513) 865-6800

Business 18
Executive Coach

What do Alexander the Great, Marilyn Monroe and King Boleslas of Poland all have in common?

They were all famous. They were all left-handed. And . . . they all had a coach.

What is a coach, exactly? A coach is an advisor. A mentor.

A coach helps you get what you want in life. Sometimes, a coach introduces you to key people who will help you get ahead. Or, a coach can help you get the position you want.

What makes a coach an *executive* coach?

Your business clients do. Usually, they are climbing the executive ladder. A coach helps them to position themselves for promotions.

Executive coaches are sometimes called *professional advisors*.

Executive coaches used to be called mentors. Mentors helped groom promising young executives in big companies.. Then, when companies downsized, mentors lost their own jobs along with everyone else. For a long time, mentors remained out of style.

Today, the executive coach has taken the place of the mentor. Executive coaching is a new and booming field.

You can easily make a high six-figure income. You are paid about the same as a psychiatrist. A typical coach works with 20 to 25 clients a month. A client stays with the coach five or six months. Some clients even return for refresher sessions.

You are not required to have a license or training.

Here's another interesting point. It's not necessary to meet clients face to face. Many coaches "meet" with their clients over the telephone or by e-mail.

Do you think you could be a successful coach?

I think you could.

SETTING UP BUSINESS

Here's how you can get into this business:
- Decide who your clients will be. The best way to do this is to specialize in a certain group of people.

Perhaps you want to work with middle managers, CEOs or sales professionals. University presidents are a good choice, too, as they tend to continuously move on to better jobs.

Only take on clients who are willing and able to pay you.

▶ Next, set up your company as an S corporation or an LLC.

▶ Order professionally designed letterhead, brochures and business cards. Open a business bank account. You will also need merchant status to be able to accept credit cards over the telephone.

➤ You should have three or four references. New clients always ask for them even if they don't check them out.

➤ Join the International Coach Federation (ICF) in Washington, D.C. Also join the Better Business Bureau.

➤ Do some research. Go to the library and read several career planning books. Access career-building sites on the Internet. Plan sessions with clients using methods you learn both in books and on the Internet.

Another excellent source is the U.S. Government. The Employment and Training Administration in the Department of Labor can tell you what jobs are in demand. Buy the inexpensive Occupational Outlook Handbook from the Superintendent of Documents. It gives detailed information on over 250 positions and it is up-to-date.

FINDING CLIENTS

◆ Advertise. Spend as little money as possible. Take out small classified ads in magazines that your prospective clients would read.

◆ Send a one-page sales letter, brochure and business card to a narrow group of prospects. Out of 1000 mailings you may receive ten clients.

This is enough to start you out.

- Give seminars on changing careers. Meet with the personnel head in major companies and offer to give a free talk on time management or selling the company's product.
- Make yourself an expert. Join the International Coach Federation. They have a referral service for their members on the Internet. Their Internet address: www.coachfederation.org.
- Set up your own Web site and advertise your services.
- Establish a meeting place. It's perfectly fine to have a home office. Arrange to meet your clients elsewhere unless you have a professional office in your home. I have found hotel dining rooms are excellent meeting places. For the price of lunch you can conduct business in the lushest surroundings.

WORKING WITH CLIENTS

How do you deal with your clients once you have them?

First, let's look at what drives people to seek advice.

Stress. People cannot count on having a job tomorrow. Health care and pensions are no longer assured.

Frustration. People love their job and are making fantastic money. But they aren't happy.

Lack of time. People are time-starved. Society is in a rush. People are running faster just to keep up.

Workaholism. Workaholics may not even like their job but it's all they've got. They end up working days, nights and week-ends.

Isolation. There's no one else to turn to. Mentors have disappeared.

Divorce. People going through divorce have a hard time just coping with day-to-day business. Their personal worries spill over into the office.

What makes the executive coach different from a consultant?

A *coach* encourages the client to do all the talking. You are there only to guide him or her. Allow the client to reach his or her own conclusion. Provide resources. Lend support.

A *consultant* hears the complaint, spots the problem and offers a solution. If the consultant is hired to play an active role, he or she takes steps to see that the problem is solved.

Some typical client problems are a lack of time and dread of public speaking. Here are a few tips on dealing with them:

Lack of time is the biggest issue for many clients.

They spend eight to nine hours at work and then bring work home. Evenings are taken up with business functions. There are business trips to Tokyo or Geneva. Finally, they lose touch with their family.

As a coach, you might conclude the problem is truly a lack of time. But don't always believe what a client says. It may turn out that he or she doesn't want to go home. The marriage is over. The work is an excuse to get away. The client will eventually tell you this.

Dread of public speaking is common to most of

us. Bring clients to Toastmasters International. This is a speakers support group. It has helped many people overcome fear of public appearances.

MAKING A FIRST IMPRESSION

Your first impression sells you. New clients judge you within the first thirty seconds of meeting you.

Work on appearing as a successful and sincere person. Even though you are excellent on the inside, you have to look like it on the outside.

The two questions that new clients most often ask themselves about you are:

"Does this person feel right to me?"

"Is this person making sense?"

SIDE BUSINESSES

- Audio tapes are a hot item. Commuters play them in the car. Find someone who knows about stress-relieving techniques and pay him or her to work with you on a tape.

    Nature tapes are also big sellers. Record waterfalls, birds chirping, the wind and the rain.

- Seminars on careers can make you very wealthy. Hire professionals to promote you. Invite speakers to share the stage with you. Have a product ready to sell such as a week's retreat in the country, video cassettes, audio tapes, CDs, books and T-shirts.

- Set up a hotline with a pay-per-call number.

People pay by the minute to tell you their dilemma and hear your advice.
- Publish a newsletter. Include job trends and useful news.

Executive coaching is going to gain popularity throughout the 21st century. Get into it now and establish yourself as a leader.

WHAT TO DO

Form an S corporation or LLC

Rent a post office box

Join the International Coach Federation

Offer your service to major companies to train executives

Advertise on the Internet

Develop a style of your own

Research current job trends

RESOURCES

International Coach Federation (ICF)
1444 I St. NW, Ste. 700
Washington, DC 20005
(888) 432-3131
www.coachfederation.org

PART III

Succeeding in Business

Marketing is Magic

What could be more magical than this:

A small classified ad for a $3.95 spatula brings you 300,000 orders and over $1 million.

This is not an isolated case. Marketers are making this kind of money.

And so can you!

Marketing is letting people know you have something of value for them.

Marketing is the most expensive part of your business. If you are selling a $5 pen, you may spend $1 marketing it. But if you sell a million pens, you'll make $4 million. And that's worth it.

You can market anything once you know how. Let's find out how.

WHAT MAKES PEOPLE BUY

Psychologist Abraham Maslow said there are five basic human needs. They are:

    Hunger and thirst
    Security

Love and belonging
Self-esteem
Self-realization

These are the motivators that make people buy.

Look at what you are selling. Does it satisfy at least one of these basic needs?

Automobile manufacturers understand basic needs. Notice how their ads play them up. If you buy the car, you find love. If you buy the most expensive car, you get the love plus money.

Cigarette manufacturers know how to fill a certain longing. Marlboro urged us to "Come to Marlboro Country." We got the idea there was a place where we belonged.

Belonging is a strong need. No one wants to be an outcast. We're made aware of this early in life. Do you remember being teased in the first grade? I do. My grandmother made me wear the sleeves cut off of my uncle's long underwear to keep my sweater arms clean. Those underwear sleeves made me an outcast. I never belonged.

One way to stimulate the need for belonging is testimonials. If other people praise your product, new buyers will want to try it. You'll be trusted.

Fear is a powerful motivator. When security is gone, fear is all that's left. Insurance companies play on fear. Burglar alarm companies do, also.

If you have a product that keeps people safe and secure, you can almost name your price by using the fear angle.

THE THREE SECRETS THE FORTUNE 500 COMPANIES ALL KNOW

Secret 1 – Target your market

Your best market are people who have money, need your product and are growing in number.

Take working couples who have pets. They don't have time to walk the dog or take him to the vet or grooming parlor. Their numbers are growing and many have quite a decent income. They would welcome a pet walking and chauffeur service.

Offer related products and services to your customers. Leashes, dog blankets, collars and taking pets' photographs are big sellers.

Secret 2 - Sell one benefit

There is a difference between the features of your product and the benefits.

A feature is the fact that your teapot has a genuine Indonesian straw handle. A benefit is that the teapot keeps the tea hot longer so the user doesn't have to reheat it.

Sell the benefit—not the feature.

Look at your product the way buyers do. They ask themselves: "What is this teapot going to do for me?"

Make one benefit your slogan.

Big companies do this. Look at Federal Express's slogan: "When it absolutely, positively has to be there overnight." These words tell you to rely on them to deliver. What a benefit!

Your slogan should be your core idea, your motto. Put it into a short sentence—no more than eleven words.

One secret to finding benefits for your product is watching trends. Look for problems. See what people are complaining about.

Three major benefits that can sell anything are:
  Saving time
  Convenience
  Service

- Saving time. People are time starved. They have no time to cook, keep house, walk the dog or even find a mate. We don't have time to take a train anymore so the trains are nearly gone. If your product saves time, let people know.
- Convenience. Does your product clean itself, require no maintenance, need no battery? Is it portable? Does it switch to another voltage so you can use it abroad?
- Service. People will pay extra for service. It means selling with a smile. Giving a guarantee. Replacing a defective product. Returning calls and having a live person answer your phone.

Secret 3 - Do what the competition isn't doing

Offer something the competition doesn't have and customers will come to you.

Here are some ideas:
  Stay open on week-ends and one hour later in the evening
  Add something of value such as a free initial appointment

Give free discounts
Hold a sweepstakes drawing
Observe the 5/12 rule: Contact customers five times in twelve months
Have a live person answer the telephone

PROMOTING YOUR PRODUCT

Promoting your product is a major part of marketing. Promotion means reaching customers. The best way of doing this is through:
Advertising
Publicity
Direct Marketing
Direct Mail

Advertising

Advertising works. It brings in orders. Advertising is expensive. Focus on the people most likely to buy.

Here are some ways to get the most for your dollar:

▶ **Keep it simple.**

Take one benefit and target a specific group of people.

Here is a sampling of ads that work:

Lost the Other Shoe? Toothache?
Call The Closet Organizers Call Dr. Gentle
(xxx) 777-7777 (xxx) 777-7777

► Set up your own advertising agency.

This is called an *in-house agency*. You receive a 15 percent discount from magazines, newspapers, radio, television and other media. There's an additional two percent off for paying promptly and price reductions for repeat ads.

The media give these discounts only to recognized ad agencies. So, make your agency separate from your regular business. Give it another name. It should have its own letterhead, business cards, business checking account and telephone number.

It's easy to place an ad. Fill out an "insertion order," and send it to the publication with the fee.

Make your own Advertising Response Sheet. Look at which ads are pulling. Focus on these. If an ad does not bring in orders after running three times, drop it. It may be a bad ad or it's appearing in the wrong place.

► Topping

Topping is placing your ad in the triangular sign on top of a taxicab. This is very effective, particularly in big cities. Contact the Taxi and Limousine Service. Make sure your taxicab works nights and has a lighted top. If the cab breaks down, you want the ad switched to another one right away. Follow up on this, making sure the taxicab goes out every day.

► *Yellow Pages*

The *Yellow Pages* are your most important advertising medium. Place your ad in the local edition and the international one. If you have a toll-free number, put it in the toll-free edition.

➤ Brochures

Hand out brochures at trade shows, seminars and speaking engagements. Send them by mail in reply to inquiries. Place them in packages you send.

➤ Flyers

Flyers are cheap and easy to distribute. The message is short. Like all good advertising, the title contains a hook, the body is about a benefit and the end is a call to action. Your name, address and telephone number should appear three times.

➤ Bus benches

A bus bench in a busy area is a perfect spot for an ad. Call up the transportation department and see if you can put an ad on the bench back.

➤ Television

Television commercials can skyrocket your sales. And, a good ad agency can make almost any product or service appear to be a compelling buy. Television advertising is expensive. Here are some ways to boost sales and keep costs down:

Use a toll-free number in your commercial.

Put your ad on local cable television. It costs much less than network television. For between $1000 and $1500 you can hire professionals to produce your spot ad.

Use *per inquiry*, or P.I., ads. This is how it works: You pay the station no money up front. They run the commercial. You keep track of the number of responses or inquiries and pay the station the agreed-upon amount for each one.

Ask for *remnant* or *stand-by* time. Contract with

a media service that has bought a block of air time. This air time is deeply discounted. You have no control over what time your commercial will air, though. And, you are given little advance warning.

➤ The Internet

On the Internet you are as big as a Fortune 500 company. The Internet gives us all an equal opportunity to get our message out. Never before has there been such a phenomenal opportunity for us to reach our public.

Marketing online is simple and inexpensive. Team up with other companies and form a mini mall. Each company would post the others' ads on its Web site.

Here a couple of tips from the pros:

Hire a professional to design your Web site and host it. Keep the information fresh so searchers return to your site again and again.

Have as many key words about you as possible appear in directories. These key words relate to your product. A potential customer would access them and see your product each time.

➤ Catalogues

If you can get your product into a catalogue with circulation of five million to ten million, you can make an enormous amount of money. A large catalogue will pretty much set the price at which they will sell your product. The price may seem low but you make up for it in volume. Check the Appendix for catalogue directories.

Publicity

Publicity is the second way of promoting your product. It is almost always free. And it can work better than high-cost advertising. Publicity means getting public exposure.

Here are a few ways to use publicity:

➤ **Networking**

Networking is getting together with others to market your product.

Here are some top ways to network:
- Business card mixers. The Chamber of Commerce holds mixers regularly. Make friends with other business owners. Exchange business cards. You may find customers among the businesses in town.
- Referral exchange. Ask people to refer customers to you and you do the same for them.
- Seminars and classes. Speakers are in great demand. Evening classes are given in all the big cities. You can hold seminars at colleges and universities on your specialty. Have news releases sent to the media stating what you are doing.
- Associations. Find associations that your potential customers belong to and ask to become an associate member. Meetings and social gatherings will give you a chance to meet people who may want your product or service.

➤ **PASS**

PASS is an opportunity to sell to the biggest buyer

in the world—the Federal Government. Each year, the government spends over $180 billion on everything from satellites to paperclips.

PASS is referral list of small businesses wishing to do business with the Federal Government. You can be on that list. Contact the Small Business Administration.

PASS is free.

➤ News Stories

Ask a newspaper or a magazine to write a story about you. Show how your business provides a solution or offers something new. Ask the feature editor to do the story, or the women's editor or the home and garden editor. They have a bigger readership than the business section has.

➤ News Release

A good news release can make you famous. It must sound like a news story. Write it as a journalist would. Keep it to one page. Answer the usual news story questions:

Who, What, Why, When and Where

The media will show up on your doorstep. Have a media kit ready to hand out.

➤ Trade Show

The trade show is a publicity extravaganza. Contact your trade association to find out when the next show is. Most are business to business events.

Plan well in advance. Send a large number of hand-written invitations to businesses that may buy your product. Draw up a list of questions to ask visitors about their business. Have small gifts with your logo ready to hand out. At least three people should be working your booth.

Rent booth space where the heaviest foot traffic is. The traffic flows from the main entrance to the center aisles and covers the right-hand side of the room. Rent the smallest booth or table and bring your own special lighting.

▶ Endorsements

Endorsements are having other people say how good you are. These include:

Word of mouth. Your customers refer others to you.

Testimonials. Other people write or talk about how much they like your product or service.

Official endorsements. An independent body such as the Better Business Bureau, the Underwriters Laboratory, or a consumers' group gives you their seal of approval.

Direct Marketing

Direct marketing is another way of promoting your product. It is meeting prospective customers face to face.

The best means are:
- Group parties
- Seminars
- Canvassing
- Dealers

▶ Group Parties

These are like Tupperware parties. Select a party

host who invites friends over to his or her house and sells your product.

Almost everyone who attends a group party is going to buy your product. All attendees should be given your catalogue and other sales material as well as a small gift.

The host receives a percentage of each sale.

➤ Seminars

Seminars have products for sale. Videos, audio cassettes, CDs, books and courses. You can hold a seminar almost anywhere. Many are held in a university, at an adult learning center or a hotel.

Giving a seminar involves speaking before a group. If this is difficult for you, hire someone with experience to do.

➤ Canvassing

Hire people to knock on doors and sell your product or service. Check with officials to see if you need a permit.

Canvassing is a dynamic way to sell products. Many people buy from door-to-door salespeople.

➤ Dealers

Dealers sell your product for you. Advertise for them in opportunity seeker publications. Put: "Dealer Inquiries Welcomed" in all advertising materials. Offer your dealers at least 50 percent discount.

Direct Mail

Direct mail is a fourth way of promoting your product. It means sending a sales letter to a name on a list. Certain products, such as newsletters, are almost always sold by direct mail.

Postage makes direct mail expensive. In addition, the price of paper has risen sharply. They are the two highest costs. Also, studies show that the response rate is one percent. That means, only ten people respond out of a thousand mailings. Not all of the ten who respond, actually buy.

However, if you have a good, tight list and your product is fairly expensive, direct mail can be excellent.

To get the most out of direct mail, use these tips:

> Use a list broker to find the best mailing list available.
>
> Send out a catalogue with only a few items in it.
>
> Hire a professional copywriter to write your sales material.
>
> Use card decks to sell a single product.

Secrets of Doubling ... or Tripling your Profits

Whatever your business, more sales are your goal. Increased sales can double or even triple your profits. There are a few simple steps that may make sales grow and keep on growing.

They include:
  Getting your sales message out to more people
  Making it easier to buy
  Selling several products

Below are seven ways you can use to put these steps into action. Other people have seen their profits soar just by using one or two of them.

You can do the same.

CREDIT CARDS

Hard cash is the best way of getting paid. Extending credit or putting people on the books is risky and can put you out of business fast.

Credit cards are a form of hard cash. You'll find your sales skyrocket when you accept credit cards. Customers are more willing to buy if they don't have to pay right away.

To accept credit cards, a person must have merchant status. Often a trade association will provide you with merchant status. Or, there are companies that will accept credit card orders for you. You pay them for the service.

TOLL-FREE NUMBER

The toll-free telephone number is pure magic. It excites potential customers. People can call you from all over the world and place an order without risking a cent. What's more, a toll-free number says that your business is big and trustworthy.

A toll-free number is easy to get. Ask your telephone company for a toll-free hook-up. You can also get an international toll-free hook-up if you are marketing goods abroad.

It's not expensive. The monthly service fee is low. The per-minute charge is also low. You may even qualify for a volume discount.

Order a custom number that describes your business. Only seven letters or numbers register with the telephone system but you can run over by one or two.

Look at some of the popular 1-800 numbers:
    1-800 MATTRESS
    1-800 LIMOUSINE
    1-800 FLOWERS
    1-800 321-PETS

To get the full benefit of a toll-free number you have to accept credit cards.

It is best to have a 24-hour, live answering service. You can sign up with a toll-free answering service.

GUARANTEE

According to studies, "guarantee" is one of the top selling words in the language. People buy when they see it.

We do not like risk. No matter how small the amount of money. We like to know we are protected. We want to know we can get our money back.

In no place is this more true than in mail order. People tend to buy on impulse. In mail order, however, they are asked to buy a product sight unseen. But, if they have any hesitation, the very word, "guarantee," overcomes it.

You won't have to return everyone's money, however. As mail order experts will tell you, customers seldom return goods even if they're not satisfied.

Here is how to get the biggest bang from your guarantee:

- Give customers a meaningful guarantee and stand by it.
- Use bold print. Make the guarantee short and easy to understand.
- Place the guarantee in all sales literature and on the order card.
- Make the guarantee look valuable, like paper money, by putting a scroll border around it.

Here are some effective guarantees:

"Our Iron-Clad Unconditional Guarantee: If Waterfall Chimes isn't everything you thought it was, just return it within 30 days for a complete refund."

"I'll buy it back! I'll buy back your inner-sound pillow for the full price you paid. No questions asked."

"$300.00 Guarantee! If this amazing Easy Time Tax Course does not save me at least $300.00 the first year or if I am not completely satisfied, I will return it within one year for a full refund."

EXPORTING

Exporting your product abroad is a goldmine. There is a mountain of prospective customers out there just waiting for you to reach them.

There will never be another time like this to sell your product around the world. New consumers everywhere are just coming into their own. They have jobs. They have money. And, they want what you're selling.

Thanks to television, people in remote corners of the world know what people are wearing in London, New York or Paris.

This reminds me of backpacking in Malaysia. I ended up in a little village at dusk and looked for a place to stay. I was told the local restaurant was renting rooms in the back.

There was no one in the restaurant when I walked in. But I heard the sound of voices in the neighboring shop. There, I found the restaurant owner and his friends. They were huddled around a television set watching an old rerun of "Dallas."

They didn't understand English and the soundtrack wasn't dubbed, but they were somehow able to follow the story. And, they were absorbed by the rich lifestyle they saw.

Those people in that village are your prospective buyers. They want the things they see on television. And there are several billion people just like them.

Think of what this means. You may sell 10 thousand pocket voice recorders in the United States this year. But you could sell six million in China.

Only a small number of companies export their goods. They are afraid of moving their products abroad. They think it's too difficult. They are convinced there's too much risk.

Take out the risk. Hire professionals to do the work. Ask the government to support you free of charge.

Here's how:

The Department of Commerce, for a small fee, will locate three agents to handle your product abroad. Get your money up front by means of an irrevocable letter of credit. Also, ask the manufacturer of your product if he or she can dropship the item.

Here are some excellent products to export:

- Electronic items
- Personal security items such as pepper spray, flashing lights that can be worn, whistles and horns, anti-theft devices for cars and bikes
- Home and business security items such as alarms, locks, smoke detectors, carbon monoxide detectors, fire extinguishers
- Small kitchen items and appliances

- Good luck charms, magical figures, crystal balls

Look in the chapters: "Import-Export" and "Your Man in Rio" for more information on doing business abroad.

SPECIALIZING

By specializing, a person focuses on a narrow group of people and offers a product to suit them.

Let's see how it works.

If you decide to market to Hispanics, you have an affluent group that's growing fast. To reach them, advertise in Spanish-language publications, on Spanish-language TV and radio or on the Internet.

Divide the market into groups. Mexicans, Cubans, Island Puerto Ricans, Mainland Puerto Ricans, Central Americans and South Americans.

Each group has its own dialect, culture and buying patterns.

Next, study each group. Learn where they live, income, household size, ages, interests and what they buy. Narrow your prospects down as far as possible.

If you sell travel accessories, your prospects might be Colombians, over the age of fifty, with an income over $60,000, who travel to Europe at least twice a year. Drug mules?

Tailor your product to suit prospective customers. This might include putting the customer's initials on items.

FRAGMENTING

Fragmenting means spinning other products or services off your main product. If, for example, you are selling a non-stick frying pan, you might offer: non-scratch utensils, an insert for deep frying, a special cook book or video.

Whatever your product or service is, it's possible to find some related product to offer. As long as you are selling one product, it costs you nothing to sell a second or a third.

At the end of each business chapter in this book is a group of side businesses. That is an example of fragmenting. Some side businesses might be more interesting than the main business. See if any of them interest you.

NETWORKING

If I had to choose just one way to make more money, it would be networking.

It's people who get you where you want to go. Business people who have everything going for them fail all the time. They have boundless energy, a sought-after product and expensive advertising.

Why do they fail? They have no network.

The ones who succeed often have a network of fifty to sixty contacts to fall back on.

Take a friend of mine as an example. He opened a pizza parlor. He did everything the business school told him. He had a brand-name product. He was located across the street from a big high school. There were office buildings on either side of him. A marketing study assured him the foot traffic was heavy right outside his door.

And, what happened?

He failed. No one came to his pizza parlor.

Why?

He had no network. No one put the word out that he was there. None of the business people in the neighborhood came in. No one helped him hang on long enough for word to get out.

Your network should include your customers, your suppliers, bankers, lawyers, accountants and local business people.

Where do you begin to start your network? Try Toastmasters International. Look up the nearest one in the phone book. They will help you address groups. But, more than that, you'll make contacts.

Join the local Chamber of Commerce and the Better Business Bureau.

Go to trade shows. If you don't want to exhibit, at least go as a buyer. You will find no end of people eager to meet you.

When you have a network of 200 or more contacts, go to a Rolodex party. Here, you can exchange the names in your Rolodex with someone else's.

CUSTOMER QUESTIONNAIRES

Be a friend to your customers. Ask their opinion about your products and services by having them fill out a questionnaire. Keep them informed about any new products you are planning. Thank them with a small gift.

Keep your old customers happy and they will keep you in business.

A Parting Thought

You can live the kind of life you've always dreamed of.

You already have all the courage and ability it takes. What you need is the right business.

Take one of the businesses in this guide and reshape it so it fits you - and what you want to do with your life. The money will come.

Whatever business you go into, you'll meet people. And people will lead you into new ventures. One business may lead to two or three others. The opportunities are out there.

Just remember to keep things simple.

Appendix

202 Make the Money and Run

Business Launching Checklist

- [x] Check the resources for the business in which you are interested.

- [ ] Write to the proper trade association for information about your business.

- [ ] Determine who your customers will be.

- [ ] Check the census data to find out where your customers are located.

- [ ] Decide which business you are going into.

- [ ] Calculate the cash needed for one year in business.

- [ ] Join a state and a national trade association for your business.

- [ ] Set up business as a sole proprietorship, a corporation, an S corporation, a limited liability company or a partnership.

- [ ] Obtain necessary licenses.

Make the Money and Run

- ☐ Open a business checking account.
- ☐ Obtain an FIN (Federal ID number).
- ☐ Obtain a state sales tax number.
- ☐ Locate a banker to do business with.
- ☐ Check zoning laws.
- ☐ Find out rules for the placement of business signs.
- ☐ Join the Chamber of Commerce or Better Business Bureau.
- ☐ Purchase business insurance.
- ☐ Set up quality telephone answering service.
- ☐ Install a toll-free telephone number for order taking.
- ☐ Open a merchant status account for charge cards.
- ☐ Write a brief business plan.
- ☐ Contact a business school about hiring graduate interns.
- ☐ Advertise on the Internet and in the *Yellow Pages*.
- ☐ Locate an accountant to handle taxes and file quarterly returns.

Publications

All-in-One Media Directory
Gebbie Press
P.O. Box 1000
New Paltz, NY 12561
(914) 255-7560

Bacon's Media Information Directories
Bacon's Information Inc.
332 S. Michigan Ave.
Chicago, IL 60604
(800) 621-0561

Business Organizations, Agencies and Publications Directory
The Gale Group
27500 Drake Rd.
Farmington Hills, MI 48331
(800) 877-GALE

Creative Sourcebook; Media Access
Sumner Communications, Inc.
4085 Chain Bridge Rd., Ste 400
Fairfax, VA 22030-4106
(703) 385-5600

Direct Marketing Association's Great Catalog Guide
Direct Marketing Association
1120 Avenue of the Americas
New York, NY 10036-8096
(212) 768-7277

Directories in Print
The Gale Group
(See above.)

The Directory of Mail Order Catalogs
Grey House Publishing
Pocket Knife Square
Lakeville, CT 06039
(800) 562-2139

Encyclopedia of Associations
The Gale Group
(See above.)

The Encyclopedia of Business Information Sources
The Gale Group
(See above.)

The Gale Directory of Data Bases
The Gale Group
(See above.)

The Gale Directory of Publications and Broadcast Media
The Gale Group
(See above.)

Guide to American Directories
B. Klein Publications
P.O. Box 6578
Delray Beach, FL 33482
(561) 496-3348

Hispanic Media USA
The Media Institute
3017 M St., NW
Washington, DC 20007
(202) 298-7512

IMS / Ayer Directory of Publications
Information Market Place
R.R. Bowker
121 Chanlon Rd.
New Providence, NJ 07974
(800) 521-8110

Kamoroff, Bernard, *Small-Time Operator.*
Bell Springs Publishing
Box 1240
Willits, CA 95490

Lant, Jeffrey. *The Unabashed Self-Promoter's Guide.*
Cambridge, MA, Jeffrey Lant Associates, 1983.

The Lawyer's Register by Specialties and Fields of Law
Lawyers Register Publishing Company
5325 Naiman Parkway
Cleveland, OH 44159

Marketing Made Easier: Guide to Free Product Publicity
Todd Publications
18 N. Greenbush Rd.
West Nyack, NY 10994
(914) 358-6213
(Over 1200 periodicals)

Marketing on a Shoestring: Low Cost Tips for Marketing Your Products & Services
John Wiley & Sons, Inc.
605 3rd Ave.
New York, NY 10158
(800) 225-5945

Martindale-Hubbell Law Directory
(Lists attorneys and their areas of specialization. This book is available at most libraries.)

National Directory of Newsletters
Oxbridge Communications, Inc.
150 Fifth Ave., #302
New York, NY 10011-4311
(212) 742-0231
(Lists 9000 North American catalogs)

National Trade and Professional Associations of the U.S.
Columbia Books, Inc.
777 14th St., NW
Washington, DC 20085
(202) 737-3777

Newspaper/Magazine Directory
Bacon's Information
332 South Michigan Ave., #900
Chicago, IL 60604
(800) 621-0561

Oxbridge Directory of Mailing Lists
Oxbridge Communications (See above.)

Pasiuk, Holly, *The Catalog Connection*
490 Three Corners Rd., P.O. Box 1427
Guilford, CT 06439
(203) 453-9701

Radio Publicity Outlets
Box 1197
New Milford, CT 06776

SRDS (Standard Rate and Data Service, Inc.)
1700 Higgins Rd.
Des Plaines, IL 60018
(800) 851-7737

Stone, Bob, *Successful Direct Marketing Methods*
Lincolnwood, IL, NTC Business Books, 1988.

Thomas Register of American Manufacturers
Thomas Publishing Co., 26th Fl.
5 Penn Plaza
New York, NY 10119-0102
(212) 695-0500

Trade Shows Worldwide

Trade Shows & Exhibits Schedule
Bill Communications, Inc.
355 Park Avenue S.
New York, NY 10010-1789
(212) 592-6200

TradeShow Week Data Book
Tradeshow Week, Inc.
121 Chanlon Rd.
New Providence, NJ 07974
(908) 464-6800

Ulrich's International Directory of Periodicals
R.R. Bowker (See above.)

210 Make the Money and Run

Resources

Advertising Mail Marketing Association
1901 N. Ft. Myer Drive, Ste. 401
Alexandria, VA 22209-1609
(703) 524-0096

American Business Women's Association
9100 Ward Parkway
P.O. Box 8728
Kansas City, MO 64114-0728
(816) 361-6621

American Consultants League (ACL)
304 Prince William St.
Princess Anne, MD 21853
(410) 651-4869

American Home Business Association
4505 S. Wasatch Blvd., No. 140
Salt Lake City, UT 84124
(800) 664-2422

American Marketing Association (AMA)
311 S. Wacher Dr., Ste. 5800
Chicago, IL 60606
(312) 542-9000

212 Make the Money and Run

The American Small Business Association
206 E. College St.
Grapevine, TX 76501-5364

DIALOG Information Services
3460 Hillview Ave.
Palo Alto, CA 94324
(800) 334-2564

Direct Marketing Association (DMA)
1120 Avenue of the Americas
New York, NY 10036-6700
(212) 768-7277

LEXIS/NEXIS
Mead Data Central
P.O. Box 933
Dayton, OH 45401
(513) 865-6800

Metro Creative Graphics, Inc.
33 W. 34th St.
New York, NY 10001
(212) 947-5100
(News release service)

National Association for the Cottage Industry
(NACI)
P.O. Box 14850
Chicago, IL 60614
(773) 472-8116

National Association for the Self-Employed (NAS)
P.O. Box 612067
Dallas, TX 75261-2067
(800) 232-NASE

National Association of Business Consultants (NABI)
9438 U.S. Highway 19 N., Ste. 101
Port Richey, FL 34668
(727) 862-1016

National Association of Manufacturers
1331 Pennsylvania Ave.
Ste. 1500 North Tower
Washington, DC 20004-1790
(202) 637-3000

National Business Association (NBA)
P.O. Box 728
Dallas, TX 75370
(972) 458-0900

National Federation of Independent Business (NFIB)
53 Century Blvd.
Nashville, TN 37214
(615) 872-5800 / (800) NFIB-NOW

National Management Association (NMA)
2210 Arbor Blvd.
Dayton, OH 45439
(937) 294-0421

Toastmasters International
P.O. Box 9052
Mission Viejo, CA 92690
(714) 858-8255
(Public speaking support group)

World Future Society
7910 Woodmont Ave.
Bethesda, MD 20814
(301) 656-8274
(Publishes *The Futurist* newsletter about future trends in business and other areas.)

214 Make the Money and Run

Government Help

Copyright Office
Library of Congress
101 Independence Ave. SE
Washington, DC 20559-6000
(202) 707-3000

Department of Commerce
14th St. and Constitution Ave. NW
Washington, DC 20230
(202) 482-2000

Environmental Protection Agency
401 M St., SW
Washington, DC 20460
(202) 206-2090

Export-Import Bank of the United States
811 Vermont Ave. NW, Rm. S-1004,
Washington, DC 20571
(202) 565-3946

Federal Trade Commission (FTC)
Pennsylvania Ave. & 6th St. NW
Washington, DC 20580-0001
(202) 326-2222
(Talk for free with a legal expert about your business.)

216   Make the Money and Run

Internal Revenue Service
U.S. Department of the Treasury
1111 Constitution Ave. NW
Washington, DC 20224
(202) 622-5000

Patent and Trademark Office
Department of Commerce
14th St. and Constitution Ave. NW
Washington, DC 20230
(800) 789-9199
(Patent and Trademark forms)

Procurement Automated Source System (PASS)
U.S. Small Business Administration (SBA)
Office of Government Contracting - PASS
Mail Code: 6256
409 3rd St. SW
Washington, DC 20416
(800) 231-7277
(Free marketing for your product or service)

Service Corps of Retired Executives (SCORE)
SBA Hotline (800) 827-5722
(Or contact your local Small Business Development Center for free or low-cost help)

Small Business Administration
409 3rd St. SW
Washington, DC 20416
(800) 827-5722

Trademark Search Library
Patent and Trademark Office
U.S. Department of Commerce
2011 Jefferson Davis Hwy, Rm. 2C08
Arlington, VA 22202
(703) 557-5813
(Research the name you choose for your business here. You can research and register your trademark, logo or slogan.)

United States Trademark Office
6 East 45th St.
New York, NY 10017

218 Make the Money and Run

Government Publications

Census and You
(Gives monthly data on trends in population, marketing research and manufacturing information.)

Commerce Business Daily
(Daily list of what the US Government is buying, who has been awarded contracts and information on surplus property sales.)

Economic Indicators
(Monthly information on unemployment, wages, prices and government action.)

Patent Office Gazette
Superintendent of Documents
Government Printing Office
Washington, DC 20402
(202) 512-1800
(Contains lists of government patents you can acquire.)

220   Make the Money and Run

Statistical Abstract of the United States
(Yearly overview of facts on everything from beekeepers to defense contractors.)

The Survey of Current Business
Superintendent of Documents
Government Printing Office
Washington, DC 20402
(Discusses current economic conditions.)

The U.S. Industrial Outlook
(Annual check-up of different industries and a forecast of what lies ahead for them.)

Glossary

ACCOUNTS PAYABLE – Money you owe.

ACCOUNTS RECEIVABLE – Money customers owe you.

ACCRUAL BASIS ACCOUNTING – Income and expenses are reported immediately, before money is collected or paid out.

ACID TEST RATIO – Ratio of cash plus liquid assets to current liabilities.

AD VALOREM DUTY – Tax equal to a percentage of an imported item's value.

ADD-ON SALE – Sale of an additional item to a customer.

ADVERTISING INSERTION ORDER – Binding contract with a publication to place an ad.

AGENT – Person or company acting on another's behalf.

AIDA – Sales formula: Catch prospect's *attention*; Stimulate *interest*; Create *desire*; Call for *action*.

AMERICAN SOCIETY OF APPRAISERS (APA) – Professional society that examines and accredits appraisers.

ARTICLES OF INCORPORATION – Details of a corporation's organization.

ASSETS – What you own.

BACKGROUND CHECK – Formal investigation of a person's personal and financial history.

BALANCE SHEET – Financial condition of your business at a moment in time.

BARTER – Exchange of goods or services without use of cash.

BENCHMARKS – Checkpoints to measure your marketing against your competition's.

BETTER BUSINESS BUREAU – Private, non profit corporation offering membership to businesses that meet their standards.

BID – Offer made by a company to supply an off-the-shelf product or service.

BILL OF EXCHANGE – (See Draft).

BILL OF LADING – Freight contract between a shipper and a transport company.

BINDING – Legally enforceable.

BLUE SKY – The good will value of a business that a business seller adds to his/her asking price.

BONDED WAREHOUSE – Warehouse authorized for storage of goods until duties are paid.

BOUNCEBACK OFFER – In mail-order, a sales offer included with order.

BREAKEVEN POINT – Point at which income equals expenses.

BROADSIDE – Poster.

BUDGET – The amount of money available for a particular purpose.

BULK MAILING – Mailing sent to anyone in a geographic area.

BUSINESS INTERRUPTION INSURANCE – Covers loss of revenue if business is shut down due to peril.

BUSINESS TELEPHONE LISTING – Listing in white pages includes entry in the *Yellow Pages* and in directory assistance.

BY-LAWS – Corporation's operating rules.

CAGE CODE – Code assigned by the Defense Logistics Service Center to companies selling to any of the Defense Agencies.

CANVASSING – Conducting a survey by knocking on doors of businesses or homes.

CAPITAL – Money and other assets.

CAPTION – Brief description of a picture.

CARD-DECKS – Packs of cards with ads sent directly to prospective customers. Also known as Card Packets, Direct-Response Postcards, Bingo Cards and Action Cards.

CARRIER – Transportation company for people or goods.

CASH BASIS ACCOUNTING – Income is reported only when collected and expenses reported only when paid.

CASH FLOW – Funds coming into and going out of your business monthly.

CASH FLOW FORECAST – Forecast of funds coming into your business and being disbursed over a specific time.

CASH FLOW STATEMENT – Shows when income will be received and expenses paid.

CASH ON DELIVERY (COD) – Customer pays upon receipt of goods.

CATALOGUE – List of goods for sale with prices and order form.

CERTIFICATE OF INCORPORATION – State's permission for corporation to operate within its jurisdiction.

CERTIFICATE OF ORIGIN – Document stating the country of origin of goods shipped.

CERTIFIED BUSINESS APPRAISER (CBA) – Accredited appraiser of businesses.

CERTIFIED BUSINESS INTERMEDIARY (CBI) – Accredited business appraiser.

CERTIFIED LIABILITY AND CASUALTY UNDERWRITER – Insurance agent specializing in liability and casualty.

CERTIFIED LIFE UNDERWRITER (CLU) – Life insurance agent.

CHESHIRE LABELS – Address labels affixed by machine.

CLASSIFIED AD – Brief ad with words and numbers. "Classified" means it appears under a specific heading.

CLOSING THE SALE – End steps of selling your product or service.

CODE OF FEDERAL REGULATIONS – Collection of all federal regulations from the Federal Register.

COLD MAIL – Direct mail received unexpectedly. See "hot mail."

COLLECT ON DELIVERY (COD) – Customer pays upon receipt of goods.

COMPILED MAILING LIST – List of prospects who have something in common.

CONSIGNEE – The person or company that receives goods sent by the shipper.

CONTACT PERSON – Authorized representative who meets public.

CONTRACT – Legally binding agreement.

COPYRIGHT – Legal protection of created work.

CORPORATION – State chartered organization that is a separate legal entity and is liable for its acts.

COST OF GOODS SOLD – Cost of acquiring or making goods.

COST PER INQUIRY (CPI) – Cost of ad divided by inquiries received.

COST PER ORDER (CPO) – Cost of ad divided by orders received.

COUPON – Certificate or chit given out by a merchant and offering a bonus such as a discount.

CROSS MARKETING – Teaming up with non-competitors to promote your business. Same as "cross-promotion."

CURRENCY FLUCTUATIONS – Appreciation or depreciation of one currency in terms of another.

CURRENT ASSETS – Assets to be used or turned into cash within a year.

CURRENT LIABILITIES – Debts due within one year.

CURRENT RATIO – Current assets divided by current liabilities. Tells how much money should be available to pay debts this year.

CUSTOMER SURVEY – Questionnaire filled out by a customer and used to measure the market for a product.

CUSTOMS – Duties levied on imports and exports.

DATE DRAFT – Order for payment by a specified date.

DEFERRED PAYMENT PLAN – "Bill me later" option offered to customers so they may pay after receipt of goods.

DEMURRAGE – Excess time taken for loading or unloading a ship.

DIRECT MAIL PIECE – A mailer sent directly to prospective customers.

DIRECT MARKETING – One on one communication with prospective customers.

DISCLAIMER – Denial of responsibility and consequential damages.

DISPLAY AD – Showcase ad with words and pictures.

DISTRIBUTION – Delivery of goods or services.

DISTRIBUTOR – Independent business person who distributes goods of manufacturers in a particular territory.

DOMESTIC CORPORATION – Corporation operating in the state where it is headquartered.

DOUBLING DAY – Day on which you receive one-half of all responses expected from a direct-mail campaign.

DRAFT – Order for payment.

DROPSHIPPING – System where you receive the order and your supplier ships it directly to customer.

DUMPING – Importing and selling goods at such a low price that local producers are undercut.

DUN & BRADSTREET (D&B) – Company that issues the most respected financial profiles of U.S. companies including their capital and credit rating.

DUTY – Government tax on imports.

ECONOMIC AND MONETARY UNION (EMU) – European trade bloc.

80/20 RULE – Rule of thumb that says 80 percent of business comes from 20 percent of customers.

ELECTRONIC MAIL (E-MAIL) – System of communicating via the Internet without phone, fax or mail costs.

ELECTRONIC MAILING LABELS – Mailing labels on diskettes or magnetic tape.

ELECTRONIC ORDER PROCESSING – Online ordering and paying by means of e-mail.

EMPLOYEE – Worker regularly on company payroll.

EMPLOYEE ASSISTANCE PROGRAM (EAP) – Company program to benefit employees such as a wellness program.

ENTREPRENEUR – Someone who sees an opportunity and sets up an organization to exploit it.

EQUITY – Net worth.

ESCAPE HATCH – Right to terminate or change agreement.

EURO – The single currency of the European Union.

EUROPEAN UNION – European trading bloc.

EXCHANGE RATE – Price of one currency in terms of another.

EXEMPT – Non taxable.

EXPENSES – Costs of operating a business and selling a product.

EX – Term used to indicate the point at which the shipper places goods at a buyer's disposal such as in EX Warehouse, etc.

EXPORT LICENSE – Government document permitting a company to export goods.

EXPORT MANAGEMENT COMPANY (EMC) – Private firm that acts as export agent for one or more manufacturers.

EXPORT TRADING COMPANY – Company that buys foreign goods to sell in its own country.

FACTOR – Company that buys another firm's receivables at a discount. Also called, "Factoring House."

FAIR PACKAGING AND LABELING ACT – Federal law regulating packaging and labeling of consumer goods.

FEDERAL INSURANCE CONTRIBUTION ACT (FICA) – Law requiring employer to withhold taxes and insurance from employee's wages.

FEDERAL TRADE COMMISSION (FTC) – Government agency that regulates advertising claims.

FICTITIOUS NAME STATEMENT or DOING BUSINESS AS (DBA) – Name of your business filed with the state.

FIDELITY BOND – Insurance placed on employees insuring employer against theft.

FINANCIAL STATEMENT – Statement of assets and liabilities. Also called, "Balance Sheet."

FIXED COSTS – Costs of operating a business independent of sales.

FOOD AND DRUG ADMINISTRATION (FDA) – Government agency that approves and regulates food and drugs.

FOREIGN CORPORATION – Corporation doing business in a state other than the one where it was chartered.

FOREIGN EXCHANGE – Credit instruments or currency of foreign country.

FOREIGN SALES AGENT – Person or firm that acts as a foreign sales representative of a domestic company.

FRAGMENTING – Splintering of markets into smaller, specialized markets. "Fragmenting a product" means offering related items.

FREE ON BOARD (F.O.B) – Price includes delivery of goods on board a vessel. This may be F.O.B. (name of port of exportation) or F.O.B. (name of port of importation).

FREIGHT FORWARDER – Company that handles shipment of exports.

FRINGE BENEFITS – Extra benefits to attract and retain employees.

GAZELLE COMPANIES – Companies that are growing swiftly.

GENERAL PARTNERSHIP – Business organization in which all partners have equal share in profits and losses.

GENERAL SYSTEM OF PREFERENCE LIST – List of tariff and quota breaks for underdeveloped countries.

GROSS PROFIT – Total revenue less total cost of sales.

GROSS WEIGHT – Full weight of shipment including packaging.

GUARANTEE – Seller's pledge that a product will perform as claimed.

HARMONIZED TARIFF SCHEDULE OF THE UNITED STATES – List of codes for imported items that show the rate of duty. It is published by the U.S. International Trade Commission.

HOT MAIL – Direct mail received by those who expect it.

HYPERTEXT MARKUP LANGUAGE (HTML) – Coding language used on the World Wide Web and read by a Web browser program.

IMPLIED WARRANTY – Warranty that exists by law even though it is not included in a contract.

IN-HOUSE ADVERTISING AGENCY – Advertiser's own advertising agency.

IN-HOUSE MAILING LIST – Business's list of its own customers.

INCENTIVE – Free gift or discount offered to a prospect to encourage him/her to buy your product.

INCOME – Revenue.

INCOME STATEMENT – Income and expenses over a set period that show a profit or loss. Also called, "Profit and Loss Statement."

INDEPENDENT CONTRACTOR – Self-employed person leasing his/her services.

INFOMERCIAL – Paid television program to sell products directly.

INQUIRY/ORDER PERCENTAGE (I/O%) – Percentage of inquiries that become sales. Divide orders by inquiries to arrive at percentage.

INSERT – An ad, such as a folder or circular that is inserted with an order.

INSOLVENT – Unable to pay debts.

INTELLECTUAL PROPERTY RIGHTS – Rights such as copyrights, patents and trademarks to use and sell a creative work.

INTEREST RATE – Charge for borrowing money.

INTERNET – Network of electronic communications. Also called, "Information Superhighway."

INTERSTATE COMMERCE – Trading across state lines.

INVENTORY – Goods or materials on hand.

INVOICE – Document describing product, value and payment terms.

IRREVOCABLE LETTER OF CREDIT – Bank document that guarantees specified payment. It cannot be cancelled or changed.

JOHNSON BOX – Box outlined by stars at the top of many sales letters and containing a short headline.

JUST-IN-TIME INVENTORY SYSTEM (JIT) – Products are obtained from the supplier as they are needed for selling.

KEY CODE – Code on ad or direct mail to identify source.

KEYSTONE – Retail price that is twice the wholesale price.

LAYOUT – Overall impact of your promotional materials.

LEAD TIME – Length of time to allow for production, delivery or work to take place.

LETTER OF CREDIT – Bank document that guarantees payment for goods within a given time.

LETTER SHOP – Outside service to sort, fold and insert components in envelope and personalize mailing by laser.

LIABILITIES – What you owe.

LIABILITY INSURANCE – Insurance covering claims against your business for bodily injury.

LIABLE – Legally responsible.

LICENSE – Government approval to perform a certain action.

LICENSING – Permission for others to produce and sell your creation for a percentage of the sales.

LICENSING AGENT – Intermediary between the product manufacturer and licensor.

LIMITED LIABILITY – Limited personal liability for business debts or actions.

LIMITED LIABILITY COMPANY (LLC) – Business structure that is a cross between a partnership and an S corporation.

LIMITED PARTNERSHIP – Partnership in which a general partner controls and operates the business while a limited partner remains passive.

LINE OF CREDIT – Bank's willingness to give you a short-term loan based on your maintaining a required balance.

LIQUIDATED DAMAGES – Damages that must be paid for breach of contract.

LIQUIDITY – Ease with which assets can be turned into cash. Also called, "Cash position."

LOSS LEADER – Item sold at a low price to attract customers.

MAIL ORDER FULFILLMENT – Processing and filling customer orders.

MANUFACTURERS' REPS – Agents of manufacturers selling goods to top buyers at chain stores.

MARINE INSURANCE – Air and sea insurance carried by the owner of shipment of goods against loss. It covers the loss in the event the carrier cannot be sued.

MARKDOWNS – Lowering retail prices to sell goods that aren't moving.

MARK-UP – Amount added to your price to arrive at a retail price.

MARKET – Most likely customers for your product.

MARKET ACCESS – Ease of entering a particular market.

MARKET MIX – Marketing strategy focusing on the type of product/service, the promotion and where the product is sold.

MARKET PENETRATION – Reaching as many people as possible within a specific market.

Make the Money and Run 231

MARKET RESEARCH – Finding out what your customers want.

MARKET VALUE – Market price of a similar item sold elsewhere.

MARKETING PLAN – Marketing mix including product, place, price, packaging and promotion.

MEDIA – Companies that sell air time or publication space.

MERCHANDISING – Packaging and presentation of products and services.

MERGE/PURGE – Method by which mailing lists are incorporated with other lists and duplicates are eliminated.

NEGOTIATION – Process of settling an issue.

NET ASSETS – Amount of assets that exceed debts.

NET INCOME (LOSS) – Profit (or loss) after expenses are deducted from net sales.

NET PROFIT – Gross profit less total expenses.

NETWORKING – Promoting your business by mixing with customers, suppliers and other business people.

NEWS MEMO – News story idea sent to the media.

NEWS RELEASE – Short news brief usually for publication in a newspaper or magazine.

NOTE – Short-term loan that is renewed every 30, 60 or 90 days.

OFF-SITE STORAGE FACILITY – Secured facility to store computer records for safe-keeping.

ONLINE – Being on the Internet.

OUTSOURCING – Farming out work to subcontractors.

OVERHEAD – Fixed costs of operating a business. Includes costs such as rent, utilities, salaries and other regular costs of doing business.

PACKING LIST – List of quantity and kind of items shipped.

PARENT CORPORATION – Corporation owning another corporation.

PARTNERSHIP – Business organization with two or more partners.

PASS (PROCUREMENT AUTOMATED SOURCE SYSTEM) – SBAs PASS list provides free listing to small businesses wishing to sell to the federal government.

PATENT – Right of an inventor to be the sole user and seller of his/her invention for 17 years.

PATENT PENDING – Application for a patent is on file. Also called, "patent applied for." A temporary patent, called a *Disclosure Statement,* is also available.

PER INQUIRY (PI)/ PER ORDER (PO) ADS – Ads run at low-cost or no-cost by the media in exchange for 40 percent to 60 percent of the proceeds.

PIERCING THE CORPORATE VEIL – In a sham corporation, creditors may pierce the corporate veil and sue shareholders.

PIGGY-BACK LABELS – Pressure sensitive labels.

POSITIONING – Establishing the image you desire in the marketplace.

PREFERENCES – Trading advantages given by importing countries.

PREFERRED CUSTOMER CLUB – Marketing device offering bonuses and discounts to customers signing up for "club membership."

PREMIUM – Incentive offered to a prospective buyer.

PRESS PACKET – Promotional material sent to the media with the goal of their covering you.

PRICE CEILING – Top price you can get.

PRICE FLOOR – Lowest price you can afford to offer.

PRO BONO WORK – Lending support, free of charge, to a social cause.

PRO FORMA INVOICE – Not a true invoice but rather one that may be possible under certain conditions.

PRODUCT – Item offered for sale.

PRODUCT LIABILITY – Insurance covering damages caused by products you sell or install.

PROFESSIONAL EMPLOYER ORGANIZATION (PEO) – Business that manages another company's employees and benefits.

PROFIT AND LOSS STATEMENT – List of income and expenses.

PROGRAM DIRECTOR – Person to contact at TV or radio station to air your message. Also called, "Service Director," or "Public Affairs Director."

PROGRAM PRODUCER – Person to contact at TV or radio station to set up an interview.

PROGRESS PAYMENTS – Payment made as each segment of work is completed.

PROMOTION – Marketing tool in which you offer a short-term bonus such as free installation, no sales tax or some other incentive.

PROPERTY DAMAGE LIABILITY – Insurance covering damage to others' property under your control.

PROPOSAL – Offer made by a person or company to supply a complex product or service. (See "Bid.")

PUBLIC SERVICE ANNOUNCEMENT – Announcement made free of charge for a nonprofit organization.

PUBLICITY – Free or low-cost advertising.

PURCHASE ORDER – Order for a seller to sell items to a buyer.

QUICK RATIO – Cash and accounts receivable divided by current liabilities. Shows how quickly you can pay your debts without further sales. Seventy-five cents to one dollar is healthy.

RECENCY, FREQUENCY, MONETARY (RFM) – Mailing list selection based on how recently customers bought, how often they bought and how much they spent.

REGISTRABLE MARKS – Protection of the right to use and sell one's work by means of copyright, trademark and patent.

RELOCATABLE BUSINESS – Business that can be operated anywhere.

REMNANT TIME/SPACE – Ads that run on air time availability or publication space available basis. They sell at a discount from a media service. Also called, "stand-by" time.

REQUEST FOR QUOTATION (RFQ) – Standard form you send to suppliers asking them to fill in terms, prices and other information.

RESALE TAX NUMBER – Business ID number allowing you to purchase goods for resale, tax-free. Also called, "seller's permit" and "resale permit."

RESPONDENT MAILING LIST – List of prospects who responded to other ads.

RETURN ON INVESTMENT (ROI) – Setting a price for an item based on the return you want from your investment.

REVENUE – Sales.

ROLL-OUT – Direct marketing method of sending sales material to everyone on a mailing list.

SALES TAX – Tax on items sold to consumers.

SELF INSURANCE – Having no insurance. You set aside a reserve fund for losses and claims.

SELF-MAILER – Mail piece that doesn't need an envelope.

SELLING DOWN – Selling an item at a reduced price to move it.

SELLING UP – Selling a higher priced item.

SERVICE CORPS OF RETIRED EXECUTIVES (SCORE) – SBA program in which retired executives offer free consulting.

"SHARPENING THE SAW" – Constantly improving what you do best.

SHIPPER'S EXPORT DECLARATION (SED) – Declaration submitted by exporter if shipment exceeds $2500 in value.

SHRINKAGE – Theft of inventory.

SIGHT DRAFT – Order for payment in which seller retains control of the shipment of goods.

SOLE PROPRIETORSHIP – Business organization owned by one person.

SPACE DEADLINE – Cut-off date for submitting an ad.

SPECIALTY PRINTER – Printer specializing in irregularly shaped pieces, tags, catalogues, envelopes, folders and brochures.

SPLIT-RUN PUBLICATION – Testing method by which a newspaper or magazine will allow you to run two different ads for a product in the same issue to find out which one "pulls."

STANDARD INDUSTRIAL CLASSIFICATION (SIC) – Codes used by the federal government to classify goods and services.

STANDARD RATE AND DATA SERVICE – Complete advertising guide.

STANDARDS – In international trade, standards are barriers in the form of technical specifications.

START-UP COSTS – Original investment in a new business.

STRATEGIC ALLIANCE – Teaming up with other businesses to jointly promote products and services.

STRATEGY – Mapping your direction and outlining a strategy to attain goals and objectives.

SUBCHAPTER S CORPORATION – Corporation in which profits and losses pass through to the shareholder's personal account.

SUBCONTRACTOR – Independent worker with his/her own tools and schedule who is hired for a particular project. Not an employee.

SUBSIDIARY – Corporation owned by a parent corporation.

SUCCESSION PLAN – Plan to transfer ownership of business to another person.

SUPPLIERS – Manufacturers, importers or distributors who supply goods.

SURETY BOND – Guarantee made by a surety company that a contractor will fulfill terms of a contract.

SWIPE FILE – File of other people's ideas you can borrow.

TAG LINE – Slogan. It appears beneath or beside a logo.

TARE WEIGHT – Weight of packing material without the goods.

TARGET MARKET – Most likely customers from key market segments.

TARIFF – Import duty.

TEASER COPY – Intriguing copy on an envelope.

TELEMARKETING – Contacting potential customers by telephone.

TERM LOAN – One to ten year loan paid off in monthly installments.

TESTIMONIAL – An endorsement of your product.

THOMAS REGISTER OF AMERICAN MANUFACTURERS – Listing of all U.S. manufacturers/suppliers and their products.

TICKLER FILE – File of prospective customers and your communications with them.

TIME DRAFT – Order for payment in which buyer takes possession of goods while putting off payment a month or more.

TIME-LIMITED OFFER – Marketing tool where you create a sense of urgency in a prospective customer to order immediately.

TOLL-FREE NUMBER – Telephone number that allows others to call you free of charge.

TOPPING – Advertising on top of a taxicab.

TRADE LIST – List of key business contacts in a foreign country.

TRADE SECRETS – Your company's information that has commercial value and that you want to keep out of others' hands.

TRADE SHOW – One to three day gathering of exhibitors and potential customers.

TRADEMARK – Legal right to a name or symbol.

TWO-STEP AD – Ad that invites reader to write or call for further information.

UNIFORM COMMERCIAL CODE (UCC) – Rules regulating sale of goods in all states except Louisiana.

UNIFORM RESOURCE LOCATOR (URL) – Your site address on the World Wide Web, for example: http://www.pretzel.com

UNIQUE SELLING PROPOSITION (USP) – A product's strongest benefit that is used as a slogan or headline.

VARIABLE COSTS – Costs tied to sales.

VENTURE CAPITAL – Financing for new businesses.

VENTURE CAPITALISTS – Persons or corporations that invest in businesses.

WARRANTY – Manufacturer's promises about the product.

WORKING CAPITAL – Current assets less current liabilities.

WORLD WIDE WEB (WWW) – Part of the Internet made up of "sites" containing information and advertising by individuals and organizations.

238 Make the Money and Run

Bibliography

Bacon's Media Information Directories. Chicago: Bacon's Information, Inc., 1999.

Connor, Dick, and Jeff Davidson. *Marketing Your Consulting and Professional Services.* New York, John Wiley & Sons, Inc., 1997.

Davidson, Jeffrey P. *Marketing on a Shoestring: Low Cost Tips for Marketing Your Products or Services.* New York, John Wiley, 1988.

Economic and Demographic Statistics. Washington, Bureau of the Census, U.S. Department of Commerce, Data User Service Division, Customer Service.

Encyclopedia of Associations. Farmington Hills, MI, The Gale Group, 2000.

Henricks, Mark. *Business Plans Made Easy.* Irvine, CA, Entrepreneur Media Inc., 1999.

Hoelscher, Russ von. *Selling Information by Mail.* Escondido, CA, Profit Ideas, 1991.

Holtz, Herman. *How to Succeed as an Independent Consultant.* New York, John Wiley & Sons, Inc., 1993.

Kamoroff, Bernard B. *Small Time Operator.* Willits, CA, Bell Springs Publishing, 2000.

Kennedy, Dan, ed. *No B.S. Marketing Newsletter.* 5818 North 7th St., Rm. #103, Phoenix, AZ 88014. (800) 223-7180.

Kremer, John. *Mail Order Selling Made Easier.* Fairfield, IA, Ad-Lib Publications, 1990.

LeBoeuf, Michael. *The Perfect Business.* New York, Simon & Schuster. 1996.

Levinson, Jay Conrad. *Guerrilla Marketing.* Boston, Houghton Mifflin, 1998.

Lewis, Herschell G. *More Than You Ever Wanted to Know about Mail Order Advertising.* New York, Prentice-Hall, 1983.

Loeb, Paul, and Josephine Banks. *Supertraining Your Dog.* New York, Pocket Books, 1989.

Luscher, Keith F. *Advertise!* Columbus, OH, K & L Publishing, 1991.

Murray, Katherine. *Home But Not Alone: The Parents' Work-at-Home Handbook.* Indianapolis, IN, Park Avenue Productions, 1997.

Oleck, Howard L. *Nonprofit Corporations, Organizations & Associations.* Englewood Cliffs, NJ, Prentice Hall, 1998.

Parkhurst, William. *How to Get Publicity (and Make the Most Of It Once You've Got It).* New York, HarperCollins Publishers, Inc., 2000.

Pinson, Linda and Jerry Jinnet. *Anatomy of a Business Plan.* Chicago, Dearborn Financial Publishing, Inc., 1999.

Poynter, Dan. *The Self-Publishing Manual.* Santa Barbara, CA, Para Publishing, 2000.

Ries, Al and Laura Ries. *The 22 Immutable Laws of Branding.* New York, HarperCollins Publishers, Inc., 1998.

Statistical Abstract of the United States. Washington, U.S. Department of Commerce, Bureau of the Census.

Thomas Register of American Manufacturers, 30 vols. New York, Thomas Publishing Company.

Ulrich's International Periodicals Directory. 5 vols. New Providence, NJ, R.R. Bowker's Database Publishing Group, 2000.

Woodall, Marion K. *Thinking on Your Feet.* Lake Oswego, OR, Professional Business Communication, 1988.

Woodward, Cheryl. *Starting and Running a Successful Newsletter or Magazine.* Berkeley, CA, Nolo.com, Inc., 2000.

Index

Accountant, 15
Address, 13
Advertising, 17, 38, 40, 42, 50, 72, 181
Advertising Made Easy, 135
Advertising Mail Marketing Association, 77, 211
Advertising response sheet, 182
Advisory board, 158
AliMed, 110
All-in-One Media Directory, 205
American Association of Exporters and Importers, 36, 62
American Boarding Kennels Association, 88, 93
American Business Women's Association, 211
American Consultants League, 211
American Culinary Federation, 126
American Grooming Shop Association, 94
American Home Business Association, 134, 211
American Institute of Philanthropy, 159
American Lighting Association, 47, 51
American Marketing Association, 77, 211
American Personal Chef Institute, 126
American Pet Boarding Association, 94

American Prospect Research Association, 159
American Small Business Association, 212
American Society of Association Executives, 159
Americans with Disabilities Act, 104
Americans with Disabilities Act Handbook, 152
Animals, 87-90, 92-94
Annual Register of Grant Support, 160
Anti-bias protection, 149
Anti-discrimination, 151
Anti-Discrimination Notice, 146, 151
Articles of incorporation, 155
Association(s), 185
Association for Information & Image Management, 165
Association of Independent Information Professionals, 165
Association of Records Managers, 165
Attorney General, 15
Audio cassettes, 188
Audio tapes, 172

Baby(ies), 37-42
Background check, 81
Background investigator, 118
Bacon's Media Information Directories, 205
Bar Association, 15
Belonging, 178

Benefit(s), 138, 153-154, 179
Bereavement facilitator, 91-92
Better Business Bureau, 15-16, 21, 94, 123, 162-163, 187
Board of directors, 155, 157
Bride and groom, 85
Brochures, 17, 183
Bus benches, 183
Business credit card, 20
Business name, 11
Business Organizations, Agencies and Publications, 205
Buy-sell agreement, 21-22

C corporation, 7-10, 157
Canvassing, 188
Capitol Hill, 147
Card decks, 189, 191-192
Catalog Collection, The, 208
Catalogue(s), 72, 75, 84, 99-100, 164, 184, 188
Catalogue design, 76, 189
Cats, 88-89
Cause marketing, 158
CDs, 99, 188
Census and You, 219
Center for International Trade, 58
Chamber of Commerce, 15-16, 21, 91, 94, 124, 152, 163, 185, 198
Charitable solicitation registration, 156
Charity, 153-155
Chef(s), 121-127
Chefs de Cuisine Association of America, 126
Civil Rights Code, Title VII, 151
Cloning, 92
Coach, 171
Code number(s), 54
Code of Federal Regulations, 148, 152
Collectibles, 5, 74
Commerce Business Daily, 219
Commercial truck theft, 115
Compass Industrial Register, 62
Compliance consultant, 150
Competition, 180
Computer, 18, 113-114
Computer security, 117
Consolidated EEO Notice, 146
Consultant(s), 117, 171
Consulting, 76, 99, 164

Consulting Opportunities Journal, 152
Convenience, 180
Cooking school(s), 123
Copyright Office, 215
CPA, 15
Crackers, 114
Creative Sourcebook; Media Access, 205
Credit cards, 20, 191-192,
Cumulative trauma disorders, 106
Customs, 60
Customs broker(s), 59

Dating service, 79-85
DBA, 8
Dealers, 188
Department of Commerce, 29, 57-58, 62, 215
Department of Labor, 169
DIALOG Information Services, 165, 212
Diary(ies), 129-135
Direct mail, 73, 123, 162, 181, 188-189
Direct marketing, 73, 181, 187
Direct Marketing Association, 77, 124, 212
Direct Marketing Association's Great Catalog Guide, 206
Directories in Print, 206
Directory of Mail Order Catalogs, The, 206
Disability Rights Education and Defense Fund, 110
Disabled, 104-105
Distributors, 16
Divorce, 171
Dogs, 88-89, 179
Dropshipping, 72
Dun & Bradstreet, 55

Economic Indicators, 219
Editing Your Newsletter, 69
80-20 rule, 4-5
Electronic bank robbery, 114
Employee Assistance Program, 103-104
Employee Polygraph Protection Act, 146
Employment and Training Administration, The, 169
Encyclopedia of Associations, 206

Make the Money and Run 243

Encyclopedia of Business Information Sources, The, 206
Endorsements, 187
Environmental Protection Agency, 215
Equal Employment Opportunity Commission, 151-152
ErgoPro, 110
Ergonomic(s), 103, 105, 108-110
European Union, 58
Executive coach(es), 167-173
Exhibitor(s), 137-143
Exhibits Directory, 143
Export-Import Bank of the United States, 61-62, 215
Export management company, 60
Export Opportunity Hotline, 57, 62
Exporter, 56
Exporting, 194-196

Fair Labor Standards Act, 146
Family and Medical Leave Act, 146
Fax, 18, 146, 148
Fear, 178
Feature, 179
Federal government, 186
Federal Minimum Wage Law, 146-147
Federal Register, 148, 152
Federal Tax Exemption, 155
Federal Trade Commission, 215
FIND/SVP, 161-162
First aid for animals, 92
Fitness program, 103
Flyers, 183
Food delivery, 125
Food Marketing Institute, 127
Foreign Trade Association, 62
Foreign trade zones, 56
Foundation Center, The, 159-160
Fragmenting, 197
Freight forwarder(s), 59-60
Frustration, 170
Fulfillment, 75
Fund raising, 158

Gale Directory of Databases, 206
Gale Directory of Publications and Broadcast Media, The, 206
General partnership, 7-8

General System of Preference List, 56, 60
Gift album(s), 37-43
Group parties, 187-188
Guarantee, 193-194
Guide to American Directories, 206
Gun permit, 117

Hackers, 114
Harmonized Tariff Schedule of the United States, 54
HazCom, 103
Hiring, 18-19
Hispanic Media USA, 207
Hollywood memorabilia, 75
Homemade booklet(s), 95-101
Horses, 89-91
How to Get Rich in Mail Order, 78
Hudson's Subscription Newsletter Directory, 69
Hunger, 172

ION, 119
IRS, 19, 154-156
Illuminating Engineering Society of North America, 47, 51
Image Consulting, 84
Import agents, 59, 62
Import-export, 53-62
Importer(s), 15
IMS/Ayer Directory of Publications, 207
Independent contractor(s), 164
Industrial espionage, 117
Information broker, 161-166
Information specialist, 163
In-house agency, 182
Insertion order, 182
Insurance, 13-14
Insurance fraud, 114
Intern(s), 10, 19-20
Internal Revenue Service, 19-20, 154-156, 216
International Air Transportation Associates, 33
International Association of Pet Cemeteries, 94
International Chamber of Commerce, 29
International Coach Federation, 170, 173
International Security and Detective Alliance, 118

244   Make the Money and Run

International trade consultant, 60
Internet, 17-18, 40, 92, 96, 170, 184,
Internet Yellow Pages, 98
ION, 119
Ireland, 34, 58
Ireland Chamber of Commerce in the U.S., Inc., 62
Irrevocable letter of credit, 56
Isolation, 171

Jewelry, 74
Journal of Commerce, The, 57, 61-62

Kiss, Bow or Shake Hands: How to Do Business in Sixty Countries, 36
Kitchen items, 74
Kits, 99
Kroll Associates, 32

Lack of time, 171
Lawsuit(s) 145, 148, 151
Lawyer, 12, 14-15
Lawyer's Register by Specialties and Fields of Law, The, 207
Lazaron Bio Technologies LLC, 92, 94
Lead time, 16
LegiSlate, 150
Letter of credit, 56
Letterhead, 16-17
LEXIS/NEXIS, 150, 166, 212
Library of Congress, 29
Lighting, 45-49, 51-52
  accent, 48-49
  ambient, 48-49
  directional, 46
  full spectrum, 49-50
  landscape, 49
  recessed, 46
  security, 49
  task, 48-49
Lighting designer, 45-46
  architectural, 46
  interior, 46
Lighting Protection Institute, 57
Lighting specialist, 45-52
Light(s), 45-52
Limited liability company, 7, 9-10, 72, 157, 168
Lobbying, 156

Love, 178

Mail order, 71, 76-78, 84
Mailing lists, 78
Mail-order Product Guide, 77
Mail Order Success Secrets, 77
Manufacturer(s), 15, 55
Marketing, 107, 177, 179, 181, 184, 187
Marketing consultant, 142
Marketing Made Easier: Guide to Free Product Publicity, 207
Marketing on a Shoestring: Low Cost Tips for Marketing Your Products & Services, 208
Martindale-Hubbell Law Directory, 15, 208
Maslow, Abraham, 177
Media kit, 186
Medicare, 150
Merchant status, 192
Metro Creative Graphics, Inc., 85, 212
Minimum wage, 149
Mixers, 186
More Than You Ever Wanted to Know about Mail Order Advertising, 77

National Association for the Self-Employed, 21, 212
National Association for the Cottage Industry, 212
National Association of Business Consultants, 213
National Association of Desktop Publishers, 100
National Association of Independent Publishers, 101
National Association of Investigative Specialists, 119
National Association of Manufacturers, 43
National Association of Professional Pet Sitters, 94
National Business Association, 124, 213
National Council of Nonprofit Associations, 160
National Directory of Mailing Lists, The, 78
National Directory of Newsletters, 208

National Federation of
  Independent Business, 21, 213
National Federation of Nonprofit
  Associations, 160
National Mail Order Association,
  78
National Management
  Association, 213
National Restaurant Association,
  123, 127
National Safe Workplace
  Institute, 110
National Safety Council, 110
National Small Business
  Association, 135
*National Trade and Professional
  Associations of the U.S.,* 208
Networking, 185, 197-198
News release(s), 91, 94, 186
News stories, 186
Newsletter(s), 62-70, 109, 173, 189
Newsletter & Electronic
  Publishers Association, 69, 101
Newspaper/Magazine Directory,
  208
Niche, 80, 162
Nonprofit, 153-160
*North American Directory of
  Ergonomic Professionals and
  Services,* 110

Occupational Outlook Handbook,
  169
Occupational Safety and Health
  Administration, 103, 108-109,
  111, 146, 151
Office, 13
Office of International Trade, 58
Offshore company, 58-59
Opportunities, 3
Organizational Meeting Minutes,
  156
Overnight courier service, 60
*Oxbridge Directory of Mailing
  Lists,* 208
Oxbridge Directory of Newsletters,
  69

Partnership, 9-10
Patent and Trademark Office, 216
Patent Office Gazette, 212
Pay-per-call, 164, 172
Per inquiry ads, 183

Pet(s), 87, 90-94, 179
Pet funerals, 91
Pet Services Annual Convention
  and Trade Show, 93
Pet Sitters International, 94
Pet sitting, 92
Pet Tech Inc., 94
Poster, 146-147
Premiums, 123, 142
*Principal International
  Businesses,* 55
Private detective, 32, 113-119
Private foundation, 154
Procurement Automated Source
  System (PASS), 185-186, 216
Promotion, 181-182
Public charity, 154
Publicity, 83, 181, 185
Publishers Marketing Association,
  101

Questionnaires, 198

Radio Publicity Outlets, 209
Registered agents, 155
Regulations, 145-152
Remnant time, 183-184
Repetitive motion injuries, 106
Reports, 99
Reptiles, 88
Resale number, 13
Research reports, 164
Restaurant(s), 121-127
Rolodex party, 198

S corporation, 7, 9-10, 72, 157, 168
Saving time, 180
Security, 177
Self-esteem, 178
Self-realization, 178
Self-publishing Manual, The, 101
Seminar(s), 170, 172
Service, 180
Service Corps of Retired
  Executives, 216
Shelf company, 59
Slogan, 179
Small Business Administration,
  62, 216
Small Business Administration's
  Office of International Trade,
  58

Small Business Exporters Association, 36, 62
Small Business Foundation of America, 57
Small Publishers' Association of North America, 101
Small Time Operator, 207
Society for Light Treatment and Biological Rhythms, 50-51
Society for Nonprofit Organizations, 160
Sole proprietorship, 7, 8
Specializing, 196
Standard Rate and Data, 67, 70, 209
Stand-by time, 183
State Analysis, Inc., 150
StateScape, 150
Statistical Abstract of the United States, 220
Stress, 170
Successful Direct Marketing Methods, 209
Succession plan, 22
Superintendent of Documents, 169
Supplier(s), 15-16, 72
Support Center of America, The, 158, 160
Survey of Current Business, 220

Telephone, 17
Television, 183
Testimonials, 187
Thirst, 177
Thomas Register of American Manufacturers, 40, 43, 72, 209
Time zones, 35
Toastmasters International, 172, 198, 213
Toll-free, 192-193
Topping, 182
Trade association(s), 5, 20-21, 140, 162
Trade Channel Newspaper, 55
Trade journals, 123
Trade secrets, 117
Trade show(s) 57, 76, 137-144, 186-187
Trade Show Bureau, 139, 143
Trade Show Exhibitors Association, 143
Trade Shows Worldwide, 144, 209

Trade Show & Exhibits Schedule, 209
Trademark Search Library, 217
Tradeshow Week, 143
Tradeshow Weekly Data Book, 144, 209
Two-step advertising, 73

Ulrich's International Directory of Periodicals, 209
Unabashed Self-Promoter's Guide, The, 135, 207
Underwriters Laboratory, 187
United Lighting Protection Association, 52
United States International Chamber of Commerce, 58
United States Trademark Office, 217
Unz & Company, 59
Updates, 146-147
U.S. Personal Chef Association, 124, 127
U.S. Industrial Outlook, The, 220

Veterinarians, 90
Video cassettes, 43
Video tapes, 83, 142, 150
Visas, 31
Vitamins, 74

Web site, 83-84, 162, 170
Wedding album, 41
Wellness, 103-111
Wellness Council of America, The, 111
Wellness consultant, 109
Wellness program(s), 103-105, 107
Wholesaler(s), 59
Word of mouth, 187
Workaholism, 171
Workstation(s), 108
World Association of Detectives, 119
World Future Society, 213
World Investigators Network, 119
World Trade Organization, 60
Writer's Digest, 97

Yellow Pages, 17, 83, 90, 116, 163, 182

> "Know what you want
> and you'll generally get it."
>
> —N<small>APOLEON</small> H<small>ILL</small>

Dash-Hill, LLC

The source for business
The source for life

Order Form

Individual and Trade Orders

- Order by Phone: 1(800) BOOKLOG toll free.
  Order 24 hours a day, 7 days a week.

- Order by Mail: Send in this order form to:
  BookMasters, Inc., PO Box 388, Ashland, OH 44805

- Order by FAX: Send this order form to:
  1(419) 281-6883

- E-mail your order: order@bookmaster.com

- Order online: http://www.atlasbooks.com

Please send me ____ copy (copies) of the book:
Make the money and run: 18 Businesses to Make You Rich.

GUARANTEE: I may return this book for a full and cheerful refund.

Ship to:

Name: _____

Address: _____

City: _____ State:____ Zip:_____-_____

Telephone: _____

e-mail address: _____

Sales tax: Please add 6.25% for products shipped to Ohio and 7.25% to Nevada.

Shipping and Handling: U.S. $3.95 for the first book, 50¢ for each additional book. International: $4.95 for the first book, 95¢ for each additional book.

Payment:

____ Check: Please make check out to: "Dash-Hill, LLC"

Credit Card: ❑ Visa   ❑ MasterCard   ❑ AMEX   ❑ Discover

Card # _____ Exp. date ___ / ___

Signature:_____

Dash-Hill, LLC

The source for business
The source for life

Order Form

Individual and Trade Orders

- Order by Phone: 1(800) BOOKLOG toll free.
  Order 24 hours a day, 7 days a week.

- Order by Mail: Send in this order form to:
  BookMasters, Inc., PO Box 388, Ashland, OH 44805

- Order by FAX: Send this order form to:
  1(419) 281-6883

- E-mail your order: order@bookmaster.com

- Order online: http://www.atlasbooks.com

Please send me ____ copy (copies) of the book:
Make the money and run: 18 Businesses to Make You Rich.

GUARANTEE: I may return this book for a full and cheerful refund.

Ship to:

Name: _____

Address: _____

City: _____ State: _____ Zip: _____ - _____

Telephone: _____

e-mail address: _____

Sales tax: Please add 6.25% for products shipped to Ohio and 7.25% to Nevada.

Shipping and Handling: U.S. $3.95 for the first book, 50¢ for each additional book. International: $4.95 for the first book, 95¢ for each additional book.

Payment:

____ Check: Please make check out to: "Dash-Hill, LLC"

Credit Card: ❑ Visa   ❑ MasterCard   ❑ AMEX   ❑ Discover

Card # _____ Exp. date ____ / ____

Signature: _____

Dash-Hill, LLC

The source for business
The source for life

Order Form

Individual and Trade Orders

- Order by Phone: 1(800) BOOKLOG toll free.
  Order 24 hours a day, 7 days a week.

- Order by Mail: Send in this order form to:
  BookMasters, Inc., PO Box 388, Ashland, OH 44805

- Order by FAX: Send this order form to:
  1(419) 281-6883

- E-mail your order: order@bookmaster.com

- Order online: http://www.atlasbooks.com

Please send me ____ copy (copies) of the book:
Make the money and run: 18 Businesses to Make You Rich.

GUARANTEE: I may return this book for a full and cheerful refund.

Ship to:

Name: _____

Address: _____

City: _____ State: _____ Zip: _____-_____

Telephone: _____

e-mail address: _____

Sales tax: Please add 6.25% for products shipped to Ohio and 7.25% to Nevada.

Shipping and Handling: U.S. $3.95 for the first book, 50¢ for each additional book. International: $4.95 for the first book, 95¢ for each additional book.

Payment:

____ Check: Please make check out to: "Dash-Hill, LLC"

Credit Card: ❏ Visa ❏ MasterCard ❏ AMEX ❏ Discover

Card # _____ Exp. date ___ / ___

Signature: _____

Dash-Hill, LLC

The source for business
The source for life

Order Form

Individual and Trade Orders

- Order by Phone: 1(800) BOOKLOG toll free.
  Order 24 hours a day, 7 days a week.

- Order by Mail: Send in this order form to:
  BookMasters, Inc., PO Box 388, Ashland, OH 44805

- Order by FAX: Send this order form to:
  1(419) 281-6883

- E-mail your order: order@bookmaster.com

- Order online: http://www.atlasbooks.com

Please send me ____ copy (copies) of the book:
Make the money and run: 18 Businesses to Make You Rich.

GUARANTEE: I may return this book for a full and cheerful refund.

Ship to:

Name: _____

Address: _____

City: _____ State: _____ Zip: _____-_____

Telephone: _____

e-mail address: _____

Sales tax: Please add 6.25% for products shipped to Ohio and 7.25% to Nevada.

Shipping and Handling: U.S. $3.95 for the first book, 50¢ for each additional book. International: $4.95 for the first book, 95¢ for each additional book.

Payment:

____ Check: Please make check out to: "Dash-Hill, LLC"

Credit Card: ❏ Visa ❏ MasterCard ❏ AMEX ❏ Discover

Card # _____ Exp. date ____ / ____

Signature: _____

Dash-Hill, LLC

The source for business
The source for life

Order Form

Individual and Trade Orders

- Order by Phone: 1(800) BOOKLOG toll free.
  Order 24 hours a day, 7 days a week.

- Order by Mail: Send in this order form to:
  BookMasters, Inc., PO Box 388, Ashland, OH 44805

- Order by FAX: Send this order form to:
  1(419) 281-6883

- E-mail your order: order@bookmaster.com

- Order online: http://www.atlasbooks.com

Please send me ____ copy (copies) of the book:
Make the money and run: 18 Businesses to Make You Rich.

GUARANTEE: I may return this book for a full and cheerful refund.

Ship to:

Name: _____

Address: _____

City: _____ State: _____ Zip: _____-____

Telephone: _____

e-mail address: _____

Sales tax: Please add 6.25% for products shipped to Ohio and 7.25% to Nevada.

Shipping and Handling: U.S. $3.95 for the first book, 50¢ for each additional book. International: $4.95 for the first book, 95¢ for each additional book.

Payment:

____ Check: Please make check out to: "Dash-Hill, LLC"

Credit Card: ❑ Visa   ❑ MasterCard   ❑ AMEX   ❑ Discover

Card # _____ Exp. date ____ / ____

Signature: _____

Dash-Hill, LLC

The source for business
The source for life

Order Form

Individual and Trade Orders

- Order by Phone: 1(800) BOOKLOG toll free.
  Order 24 hours a day, 7 days a week.

- Order by Mail: Send in this order form to:
  BookMasters, Inc., PO Box 388, Ashland, OH 44805

- Order by FAX: Send this order form to:
  1(419) 281-6883

- E-mail your order: order@bookmaster.com

- Order online: http://www.atlasbooks.com

Please send me ____ copy (copies) of the book:
Make the money and run: 18 Businesses to Make You Rich.

GUARANTEE: I may return this book for a full and cheerful refund.

Ship to:

Name: _____

Address: _____

City: _____ State:____ Zip:_____-_____

Telephone: _____

e-mail address: _____

Sales tax: Please add 6.25% for products shipped to Ohio and 7.25% to Nevada.

Shipping and Handling: U.S. $3.95 for the first book, 50¢ for each additional book. International: $4.95 for the first book, 95¢ for each additional book.

Payment:

____ Check: Please make check out to: "Dash-Hill, LLC"

Credit Card: ❑ Visa   ❑ MasterCard   ❑ AMEX   ❑ Discover

Card # _____ Exp. date ____ / ____

Signature: _____

Dash-Hill, LLC

The source for business
The source for life

Order Form

Individual and Trade Orders

- Order by Phone: 1(800) BOOKLOG toll free.
  Order 24 hours a day, 7 days a week.

- Order by Mail: Send in this order form to:
  BookMasters, Inc., PO Box 388, Ashland, OH 44805

- Order by FAX: Send this order form to:
  1(419) 281-6883

- E-mail your order: order@bookmaster.com

- Order online: http://www.atlasbooks.com

Please send me ____ copy (copies) of the book:
Make the money and run: 18 Businesses to Make You Rich.

GUARANTEE: I may return this book for a full and cheerful refund.

Ship to:

Name: _____

Address: _____

City: _____ State:_____ Zip:_____-_____

Telephone: _____

e-mail address: _____

Sales tax: Please add 6.25% for products shipped to Ohio and 7.25% to Nevada.

Shipping and Handling: U.S. $3.95 for the first book, 50¢ for each additional book. International: $4.95 for the first book, 95¢ for each additional book.

Payment:

____ Check: Please make check out to: "Dash-Hill, LLC"

Credit Card: ❏ Visa ❏ MasterCard ❏ AMEX ❏ Discover

Card # _____ Exp. date ____ / ____

Signature:_____